W9-BRX-145

LEA & FEBIGER   1785 – 1985

This year our firm celebrates its 200th year in business. On this occasion we greet you, friends old and new, who have contributed to the growth and success of our firm.

For your enjoyment and interest, this book takes you on a brief tour of our firm from the year we were founded up to the present.

As we stop for a moment and reflect on this anniversary, we look forward to a continued and renewed association with you in the challenging years ahead.

January 25, 1985

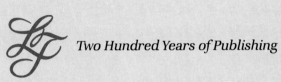 *Two Hundred Years of Publishing*

The Lea & Febiger Building on Washington Square

R. Kenneth Bussy

Two Hundred Years of Publishing

A history
of the oldest publishing
company in the United States
Lea & Febiger, 1785–1985

Lea & Febiger • Philadelphia
1985

Lᴇᴀ & Fᴇʙɪɢᴇʀ
600 Washington Square
Philadelphia, PA 19106
U.S.A.
(215) 922-1330

Library of Congress Cataloging
in Publication Data

Bussy, R. Kenneth.
  Two hundred years of publishing.

  Bibliography: p.
  Includes index.
  1. Lea & Febiger (Firm)—History.   2. Publishers
and publishing—Pennsylvania—Philadelphia—
History.   I. Title.
Z473.L45B87   1985   070.5'09748'11   84-11308
ISBN 0-8121-0947-3

Copyright © 1985 by Lea & Febiger. Copyright
under the International Copyright Union. All
Rights Reserved. This book is protected by
copyright. No part of it may be reproduced in any
manner or by any means without written
permission from the Publisher.

Printed in the United States of America

Preface

This year, 1985, is Lea & Febiger's 200th birthday. While this is a noteworthy achievement for America's oldest publisher, it is made more remarkable by the fact that the firm, beginning as a sole proprietorship, evolved into a series of partnerships and remains a partnership today, still in the hands of the descendents, by blood or marriage, of the founder, Mathew Carey.

Partnerships are a volatile business arrangement and the uncertainties are particularly enhanced by the speculative and changeable nature of publishing. Nonetheless, Lea & Febiger has managed to survive its internal problems, the comings and goings of partners, the vicissitudes of the marketplace, the disruptions of wars and depressions, the buying-up of family-owned businesses by great corporations, and more recently, a dramatic increase in the number of competitors entering the field of medical publishing.

Lea & Febiger's vigor and longevity are a tribute to the extraordinary men who shaped its history. Many of the early partners were men of national prominence, pioneers in publishing practice, and powerful voices in their community. Later partners, while not obtaining the prominence of their remarkable ancestors, have earned recognition for their shrewdness, industry, and dedication to the family business, which kept the company prosperous and its employees happy while bringing thousands of good medical titles into the world. This modest, anecdotal account is told largely in terms of those men who made the history, rather than in terms of company policies and profits.

Two Hundredth Anniversary

R. KENNETH BUSSY
Philadelphia, PA

Acknowledgments

Much of the information in this book was gathered
from an earlier volume that the company published
on the occasion of its 150th anniversary. The author
of that volume is believed to have been Van Antwerp
Lea, who expanded on a still earlier publication of
the 100th anniversary by Henry C. Lea.

Additional information was gleaned from Tebbel's
two-volume *A History of Book Publishing in the
United States*, a work of impressive proportion.
Kaser's *The Cost Book of Carey & Lea* was most
helpful, as was Bradsher's *Mathew Carey*. Material
on Parson Weems was taken largely from an article
written by Morris Bishop in 1936 in *The New Yorker*
magazine and from a publication of Weems' letters.
I also used material from various dictionaries of
biography and from Alice Johnson's unpublished
A Rage for Reason: A Study of Mathew Carey, and
had the pleasure of reading some of the writings of
Mathew Carey and Henry C. Lea. Some records and
documents concerning the firm which are to be

found in the Historical Society of Pennsylvania and in the company's own archives were consulted, as well as material at the American Antiquarian Society in Worcester, Massachusetts.

Professor Francesco Cordasco, who contributed a chapter to the book, was most helpful in giving me guidance and suggesting sources of information.

Two Hundredth Anniversary

The present partners at Lea & Febiger were supportive in providing information about their forebears, and the entire manuscript was read for style, grammar, continuity, and construction by Mrs. Dorothy DiRienzi, the manager of the Copy Editing Department at Lea & Febiger. Howard N. King designed the book, and did it well.

My secretary, Miss Sandra Davis, typed, retyped, and typed again the manuscript with her usual efficiency and good humor.

We owe a debt of gratitude to the following for the use of photographs: To the College of Physicians of Philadelphia, for the photographs of Austin Flint, Robley Dunglison, and S. Weir Mitchell; to the governors of St. George's Hospital for the photograph of Henry Gray and his classmates; to the American Antiquarian Society of Worcester, Mass., for the advertising piece used by Weems. The photograph of Henry Charles Lea is a portrait by Vonnah in the Henry C. Lea Library of the University of Pennsylvania. The photographs on the front endpapers and on page 111 are reproduced by courtesy of CONCEPTS Magazine, copyright © Wang Laboratories, Inc., 1982.

R. K. B.

Contents

Two Hundred Years of Publishing

Mathew Carey

In the Beginning: Mathew Carey

I

In the beginning there was Mathew Carey, an extraordinary, energetic, opinionated, vituperative, and able Irishman, who ran afoul of the British authorities and eventually fled his native land. Carey, born in Dublin in 1760, the year that George III ascended the British throne, was the son of a well-to-do baker. His schooling was ordinary, though he developed an insatiable appetite for reading, and at the age of 15 decided to go into printing and the related fields of publishing and bookselling.[1] At 19, Carey wrote an article in the *Hibernian Journal* that forcefully argued against dueling. At 21, he advertised an indiscreet pamphlet, which was never published, attacking the Penal Laws, and this angered the British overlords of Ireland and some of the Catholics of Dublin as well.[2] To avoid prosecution, Carey hurried off to France, where he found work in a print shop owned by Benjamin Franklin, who had been sent to France by the Continental Congress. Carey was not in Franklin's employ for very long, perhaps a month or two. His *Autobiographical Letters* contain a cryptic comment concerning

Franklin's "not having occasion for me any longer." It appears that Franklin never warmed to Carey despite Carey's public praise and endorsement of Franklin many years later. Carey, displaying his usual resiliency, soon found employment with the Didot Press, an innovative concern of prominence in French printing and publishing, and in the course of almost a year's employment, he learned a considerable amount about printing.

Two Hundredth Anniversary

He returned to Ireland in 1782, and once again his acerbic pen got him into trouble with the authorities. He spent a short time in jail and upon his release fled to Philadelphia, disguised as a woman to avoid the watchful British port authorities. He arrived in Philadelphia in 1784, after briefly considering settling in Baltimore or New York.

Carey's autobiography tells us that he arrived in Philadelphia "with but a few guineas" in his pocket,[3] and, of course, with his ever-present limp, which the same source describes as having occurred at the age of one because of the carelessness of a nurse. Fortunately the Marquis de Lafayette, whom Carey had met in France, was visiting George Washington at the time and learned of Carey's circumstances. Lafayette sent him $400, and with this slender capital, he at once established *Carey's Pennsylvania Evening Herald* on Tuesday, January 25th, 1785.[4] That is the date to which we trace Lea & Febiger's beginnings.

Carey's paper published the debates of the House of Assembly from notes that he himself took with a shorthand of his own invention. This endeavor

Marquis de Lafayette

proved quite profitable, and the new immigrant became a figure of importance in Pennsylvania.

Two Hundredth
Anniversary

On November 9, 1785, in the *Pennsylvania Evening Herald*, Carey, responding to a letter published in a rival newspaper, the *Independent Gazetteer*, made some uncomplimentary remarks about the *Gazetteer's* editor and publisher, the ex-Revolutionary War officer, Colonel Eleazer Oswald. Oswald, in turn, launched several attacks on Carey's views and Carey's friends, which led Carey, despite his aversion to dueling, to challenge the Colonel, with disastrous results.[5] Carey was badly wounded in the duel and took 15 months to recover.

Carey's friends condemned Oswald, who as an ex-soldier was far better acquainted with weapons than Carey, but Carey defended Oswald, and that, strangely enough, led Carey's friends to attack Carey. He had been in the newly formed United States but a year and was already the center of controversy and the wounded victim of a duel. Controversy was part of Carey's life, and he never shrank from it.[6] Alice Johnson, in the unpublished *A Rage for Reason: A Study of Mathew Carey*, claims that "Carey envisioned himself as a poor but honest man who by superior efforts had overcome incredible odds and garnered a tidy fortune, the proper reward for virtuous industry." He also felt that it was his duty to educate his fellow citizens "by a most liberal and vituperative use of his pen." Throughout his life he was quick to abandon his work for weeks at a time to engage in furious bouts of composition on a wide variety of subjects, resulting in a flood of pamphlets.

On March 26, 1785, Mathew Carey entered into a partnership with Christopher Talbot and William Spotswood. During Carey's life and still, to this day, the firm he founded has been individual proprietorships or a succession of partnerships. In August, 1786, Carey joined with Spotswood, Thomas Seddon, Charles Cist, and John Trenchard to establish *The Columbian Magazine,* the most handsome periodical of its day, but not the most successful. Carey withdrew from this partnership in December, 1786, and *The Columbian Magazine* folded. On January 13, 1787 Carey announced in *The Pennsylvania Evening Herald* that he was founding a magazine called *The American Museum.* This magazine became a favorite periodical for George Washington, Dr. Benjamin Rush, John Dickinson (who had signed the Declaration of Independence on behalf of Pennsylvania), and many other prominent citizens of the day. Carey was particularly fond of his brainchild, although its financial success was not equal to its artistic success, and Carey was constantly in debt. He reluctantly closed the magazine in December 1792, mostly because the post office disallowed second class mail.

In a letter written on November 9, 1789, to his brother, Thomas, who lived in Dublin, Carey noted that he meant "to go pretty much into the book business next year" and asked his brother to obtain a consignment of good and saleable titles such as classics, travel books, law books, and books of science. He noted that "Bibles are in great demand." As usual, Carey had a problem obtaining the money to carry out his plans, and he entered into another partnership—this time with a printer,

Peter Stewart. Stewart was as penurious as Carey, and the firm of Carey, Stewart & Company was a failure from the start, causing Carey to write a friend in Dublin, "I am in partnership with a Mr. Stewart, a young man whom I took without a shilling, in hopes of lightening my burden . . . I have experienced little or no assistance from him and he assumes a much greater degree of consequence than I ever pretended to. Thank God our connection is to continue only a [few] months more. Would to heaven it were at an end today."

By far the most important work to be published under the imprint of Carey, Stewart, & Company was a translation of the Catholic Rheims-Douay Bible, placed on sale in December, 1790. This came about because the Reverend John Carroll, soon to be appointed the Roman Catholic Bishop of the United States, pressured a reluctant Carey to produce a Bible for his fellow Catholics in the United States. The success of the Catholic Bible led Carey to publish a Protestant Bible a few years later. Carey paid an editor $1,000 to collate 18 different editions of Protestant Bibles in an effort to make the Bible as authentic as possible. The type for the "Carey Bible" was kept standing for 25 years for numerous printings, which helped to build Carey's considerable fortune.

There was more to Carey's life than acrimony, clashes with authority, and failed magazines. In 1791 he married Miss Bridget Flahavan,[7] daughter of an American citizen who had lost all his money in the Revolution. Bridget was poor and Carey wasn't much better off at the time, noting that he had a few odd volumes of his failed magazines and some furniture that was probably not worth $100. Nonetheless, they had something better than money: an evidently happy marriage that lasted 39 years and produced 9 children, including the remarkable Henry Charles Carey, who became an important American political economist after leaving his father's book business.

In a short time that book business flourished, and Mathew Carey became the foremost publisher in the United States as well as an innovator of marketing and promotional policies in publishing, many of which remain to this day. Among the most popular books of Carey's period were Weems' biographies of Washington and Marion, Jefferson's *Notes on Virginia*, Lavoisine's *Atlas*, the *American Atlas*, Bonaparte's *American Ornithology*, East's *Reports*, Guthrie's *Geography*, Carey's own account of the yellow fever epidemic of 1793,[8] and the only quarto Bibles manufactured in America, which Carey supplied in both the Douay version and the "Authorized Version" in various bindings. Early on, Carey began importing books from England, while at the same time encouraging American writers. Carey, and later his son, published such native writers as James Fenimore Cooper, Washington Irving, Edgar Allan Poe, the poet Philip Freneau, Noah Webster, William Gilmore Simms, and the popular novelist, Mrs. Rowson, who wrote *Charlotte Temple*, which sold over 50,000 copies. Among the more famous British writers published by Carey and his successors were Sir Walter Scott and Charles Dickens. The firm also published the tales of *Cinderella* and *Frankenstein*. It is clear from studying the books published by Carey that he had eclectic interests. In addition to his large turnout of

Two Hundredth Anniversary

9

Carey's Pennsylvania Evening Herald

bibles, atlases, novels, medical books, political works, and Weems' questionable biographies, he was in sympathy with the revolt of Spain's Latin American colonies and published several Spanish language books and a Spanish dictionary. The firm had an agent in Gibraltar in 1822, which would seem to indicate that Spanish books were being imported for the Latin American market.

The success of Carey's firm transformed the penurious Carey into a man of affluence. In 1824, on the occasion of Lafayette's second visit to the United States, Carey returned to the general the $400 so kindly given him in 1784.

In 1817 Carey brought his eldest son, Henry C. Carey, into the business, and changed the name to M. Carey & Son. This was still another of numerous changes of name that continued through 1908. Four years later, Isaac Lea, who had married Carey's daughter, Frances, joined the firm. Carey, who had been on hand to open his business each morning for years, began to devote more time to his many other interests. On January 1, 1822, Mathew Carey retired from business, leaving the firm to Henry C. Carey and Isaac Lea. The financial arrangements under which Henry and Isaac took over and operated the firm were, according to David Kaser, among the most complex in the history of legitimate business. Mathew and son Henry, two of the period's leading economists, put their heads together and evolved a contract that not only troubled the principals for more than a decade, but also puzzled a prominent Philadelphia lawyer, Horace Binney, who in 1835 was called in to arbitrate the continuing financial misunderstandings between father and son. Binney's decision was sufficiently equivocal to satisfy both parties. Essentially it gave Henry more control over the family capital while giving Mathew a larger annual income. Despite Mathew's expenditures on the many pamphlets he published and his generous gifts to charity, he apparently lived quite comfortably, as did Henry.

In describing Mathew Carey's business career, I have tended to slight his role as a patriotic and socially involved citizen. He turned out a stream of pamphlets in defense of such diverse groups as the seamstresses employed by the Army to make shirts (Carey insisted they receive a living wage) and the poor of Philadelphia, whom he defended against charges of idleness and dissipation. He wrote sympathetic pamphlets about the Poles. He also wrote on agriculture and prison discipline as well as banking policy, the need for a college in Philadelphia, the colonization of Liberia, and in support of the Chesapeake-Delaware Canal. He was strongly in favor of protecting new American industries through a high tariff, and wrote and spoke extensively on that subject. Carey himself felt that his most important writings were *Vindiciae Hibernicae*,[9] which was a rebuttal to some unfavorable and inaccurate histories of Ireland published in England, and *The Olive Branch*. The latter was published and republished time and again. It was an important work calling for an end to the intense bitterness between the Democrats and the Federalists, which resulted from radically different opinions about the War of 1812. These differences threatened the country with turmoil close to civil war. The Tariff of 1828 again caused

Carey's cancelled check to Lafayette

bitter feelings, and once again Carey fired off another pamphlet calling for peace and understanding; this one was called *Prospects on the Rubicon*. Between 1819 and 1832 Carey wrote so many pamphlets on the high tariff question that there is no telling how many hundreds he produced. In 1832 he wrote *The Crisis: An Appeal to the Good Sense of the Nation Against the Spirit of Resistance and Dissolution of the Union*. In addition to his pamphlet writing, Carey carried on an extensive correspondence with the leading politicians and thinkers of the day, all without neglecting his book business.

Carey began the first publisher's trade association, which unfortunately failed after a few years. He founded both the Hibernian Society and the first Sunday School Association in the United States. He was made a member of the Board of Health of Philadelphia in 1794. Later in life he became a director of the Bank of Pennsylvania, and was a charter member of the Philadelphia Society for the Promotion of National Industry. He also hired the first proofreader in the book business[10] and set up itinerant salesmen, such as Parson Weems, who will appear again in these pages.

Carey retained his vigor into old age despite a cough that troubled him from time to time. He was severely injured when his carriage overturned on Spring Garden Street and he died a few days later on September 16, 1839. A newspaper reported that on the day he was buried, "the streets were thronged with sad-faced spectators and thousands followed Mr. Carey to his grave with grief for his loss and reverence for his worth." Carey was originally

Isaac Lea

buried in St. Mary's church in Philadelphia, but years later his remains were placed in Holy Sepulchre Cemetery in Montgomery County, Pennsylvania.

Carey left behind thousands of letters, a journal, and a sketchy autobiography. Dipping into these writings, one concludes that he was a passionate, argumentative, and many-faceted man with a sense of humor and a zest for life. Many years later, in an 1846 speech before the American Philosophical Society, his partner, Isaac Lea, described Carey as "cheerful and animated, fond of the society of his friends, he contributed an unusual share of the conversation which was usually sprinkled with appropriate references, citations, and quotations from ancient and modern history as well as the classical poets—Horace was his book of books." One could also conclude that Carey was an injustice-collector, on the defensive against a host of real and imagined enemies. Not very much is known about his personal habits, although Arnold Green, the biographer of Henry Charles Carey, notes that "Carey was an ardent addict of the grape like his father." This is highly questionable, since Mathew Carey was the president of the local temperance society. Carey claims in his autobiography that he never entered places where drinks were served.

Personality aside, Carey is remembered as an eminently successful businessman, a patriot, a friend of formative American manufacturing, a propagandist for a balanced and powerful American economy, a patron of the arts, a friend of science, an innovator, a powerful Catholic layman, a liberal and fearless supporter of the poor and unfortunate,[11] and finally, most importantly, the greatest publisher of his day.

Two Hundredth Anniversary

NOTES

1. In the eighteenth century and well into the nineteenth century, it was common for printers to be publishers and booksellers as well.

2. In his seventy-third year, Mathew Carey was invited by the editors of the *New England Magazine* to write a series of autobiographical letters for publication in that journal. The dates Carey gave for his article in the *Hibernian Journal* and for the announcement about his pamphlet attacking the Penal Laws (which never was published) were incorrect. The announcements in the *Dublin Evening Post* and the *Dublin Journal* were dated November 10, 1781. That means that Carey was 21 at that time, not 19 as he had said. Alice Johnson has photocopies of the Dublin papers of this date.

3. Carey's autobiographical letters written to the *New England Magazine* were later gathered together in book form. While the autobiography gives some insights into Carey's personality (for example, it shows that he definitely had a sense of humor and was in no way pompous), it tells little about his personal life or inner feelings. The autobiography evidently impressed Edgar Allan Poe, who in the March, 1836, issue of the *Southern Literary Messenger*, wrote the following: "We have been delighted with the perusal of this book and consider it one of the most instructive as well as one of the most amusing of autobiographies. The ruling feature of the work is candor—a candor of the noblest description. There is much in these memories of Mr. Carey which will bring to the mind of the reader Benjamin Franklin, his shrewdness, his difficulties and his indefatigability."

4. Carey began the publication of *Carey's Pennsylvania Evening Herald* "at the fifth door south of Spruce Street on the east side of Front Street." He called the publisher M. Carey & Company.

PRIVATE LIBRARY

VINDICIÆ HIBERNICÆ;

OR,

IRELAND VINDICATED:

AN ATTEMPT TO DEVELOP AND EXPOSE A FEW OF

THE MULTIFARIOUS ERRORS AND MISREPRESENTATIONS RESPECTING IRELAND,

IN THE HISTORIES OF

MAY, TEMPLE, WHITELOCK, BORLACE, RUSHWORTH, CLARENDON, COX, CARTE, LELAND, WARNER, MACAULEY, HUME, AND OTHERS:

PARTICULARLY IN

THE LEGENDARY TALES

OF

THE PRETENDED CONSPIRACY AND MASSACRE OF 1641.

———

BY M. CAREY,

MEMBER OF THE AMERICAN PHILOSOPHICAL SOCIETY, AND OF THE AMERICAN ANTIQUARIAN SOCIETY, AUTHOR OF THE OLIVE BRANCH, ETC., ETC.

THIRD EDITION, ENLARGED AND IMPROVED.

I can truly say, that of all the papers I have blotted, which have been a good deal in my time, I have never written anything for the public without the intention of some public good. Whether I have succeeded or not, is not my part to judge.—Sir WILLIAM TEMPLE.

There is not a national feeling that has not been insulted and trodden under foot; a national right that has not been withheld, until fear forced it from the grasp of England; or a dear or ancient prejudice that has not been violated, in that abused country. As Christians, the people of Ireland have been denied, under penalties and disqualifications, the exercise of the rites of the Catholic religion, *venerable for its antiquity; admirable for its unity; and consecrated by the belief of some of the best men that ever breathed.* As men, they have been deprived of the common rights of British subjects, under the pretext that they were incapable of enjoying them: which pretext had no other foundation than their resistance of oppression, only the more severe by being sanctioned by the laws. *England first denied them the means of improvement; and then insulted them with the imputation of barbarism.*—PAULDING.

———

PHILADELPHIA:

R. P. DESILVER, 255 MARKET STREET.

1837.

The title page of Carey's 1837 Vindiciae Hibernicae

He occupied various addresses on Front Street until 1793, when he established his business at 118 High Street (now Market), on the south side of the street between Franklin's Court (now Orianna Street) and Fourth Street. In 1814 he moved to 121–124 Chestnut, and in 1830 was located on south Fourth Street at Chestnut. In 1865 Henry C. Lea erected a building at 706–708 Sansom Street; later 710 was added. In 1923–1924 the present firm erected a new building at 600 Washington Square, which it continues to occupy.

5. Oswald made several gross attacks against foreigners, which led Carey to attack Oswald. Oswald wrote, "Your being a cripple is your main protection." That did it. Carey challenged, and the duel was fought in New Jersey. Carey took a couple of glasses of wine to steady himself; he admitted that he had to screw up his courage. Before pacing off, Oswald graciously agreed to forget the challenge, but Carey insisted on going through with it and took a bullet in his thigh, which apparently led to complications because he was laid up for 15 months.

6. One of Carey's famous controversies pitted him against fiery William Cobbett, publisher of *The Political Censor* and later *Porcupine's Gazette and Daily Advertiser.* Cobbett wrote a pamphlet that vigorously attacked Dr. Joseph Priestly, the discoverer of oxygen and Unitarian clergyman, who had recently emigrated to the United States. The printer, Thomas Bradford, refused to print it and Cobbett took it to Carey, who also wanted nothing to do with it. Carey went out of his way to avoid an argument with Cobbett, for he had a healthy respect for Cobbett's invective. Nonetheless, a Cobbett supporter, John Ward Fenno, described by Carey as a "rash, thoughtless and impudent young man," launched an attack on Carey, which eventually led Carey and Cobbett into printing broadsides against each other. This feud culminated in 1799 when Carey published *The Porcupinead; a Hudibrastic Poem.* Cobbett, not content with political controversy, challenged Benjamin Rush's method of curing yellow fever by bleeding, and though he probably was right, he was sued for libel and lost. He returned to England in 1800 and 15 years later, having changed his political views, cooperated with Carey in pointing out and opposing the reactionary tendencies that followed the Congress of Vienna.

7. Before marrying Bridget Flahavan, Carey had a brief infatuation with a Miss Boys. He notes in his autobiography that "I was two or three times in company with a young lady, a Miss Boys of considerable attractions with whom I was somewhat smitten. Her charms were, I confess, more personal than intellectual, but it is generally known that at 24 or 25, the biped, man, more generally chooses a partner of the other sex by the eye than by the ear." Carey made overtures to Miss Boys' father but was rudely treated. "My Irish blood was roused," said Carey, and he showed no further interest in Miss Boys.

Two Hundredth Anniversary

8. Carey's account of the yellow fever epidemic is entitled *A Brief Account of the Malignant Fever Which Prevailed in Philadelphia in the Year 1793*. The work went into four editions in three months and sold 10,000 copies in English, in addition to which it was translated into German, French, Dutch, Spanish, and Italian. Carey also published Benjamin Rush's book on yellow fever, but Carey's suspicion that the scourge was imported from the West Indies was more correct than Rush's theory that it arose spontaneously from decaying vegetable matter. The actual cause of yellow fever remained a matter of speculation until 1900, when the controlled experiments in Cuba by the U.S. Army Yellow Fever Commission, under Walter Reed, Caroll, Lazear, and Agramonte, provided conclusive proof that the mosquito *Aedes aegypti* was the transmitting agent. Carlos Finlay had hypothesized as much in a speech in 1881, and committed his hypothesis to print in 1886 in the *American Journal of the Medical Sciences*, which was a publication of one of the Carey successor firms.

9. Carey worked hard on *Vindiciae Hibernicae* and made many changes in the text. Mrs. Bailey, the printer, charged Carey for 463 hours of author alterations at 30 cents an hour, which amounted to $138, whereas composition charges were but $369. The work, published in March, 1819, afforded Carey "as much heart-felt satisfaction as anything I have ever done, not excepting the defense of the protecting system, and the publication of *The Olive Branch.*

10. Samuel Lewis, a man of several talents including mapmaking and drafting, was hired by Carey about 1794 and

continued with him until 1816. Lewis charged Carey 25 cents per sheet proofed (67 cents a sheet for Bibles). Jesse Waterman, John Lithgow, John M. Robinson, William Christie, and Lewis C. Vallon all read proof for Carey. The nineteenth century was well advanced, however, before any publisher could afford to hire a full-time proofreader.

11. The obituary in *The Philadelphia Gazette* stated, "The cry of the poor, the widow, and the orphan was never in vain at his door. He had a hand open as day to melting charity." *The Philadelphia Inquirer* voiced similar sentiments.

Two Hundredth Anniversary

Mason Locke "Parson" Weems

"With Moral Tales & Bible Sales
He Gained an Earthly Glory-O"

II

Mason Locke "Parson" Weems played an important role in the early history of this firm as one of the itinerant salesmen that Carey hired; he was, by far, the best known. Just as the country gentry and the country bumpkins found "Mother Carey's chicken," as Weems called himself, irresistible, so do I.

Weems was born in Anne Arundel County, Maryland, in 1760. He was the youngest of David Weems' 19 children, and was educated in Latin, Greek, English, French, mathematics, merchants' accounts, and writing at what has since become Washington College, Chestertown, Maryland. He went to England at the age of 14 to study medicine at London and the University of Edinburgh. Though he is referred to in several documents as "Doctor" Weems and apparently graduated, there is no evidence that he ever practiced medicine.

Soon after his return home he once again set off for England to obtain priesthood in the Church of England. The Revolution had severed the American Episcopal Church from its parent church in

England, and the English prelates refused the benefits of the apostolic succession to American rebels. Weems and a fellow candidate, Edward Gantt, appealed to Benjamin Franklin in Paris and to John Adams in The Hague. In time the English episcopacy underwent a change of heart, and both Weems and Gantt were ordained by the Archbishop of Canterbury on September 12, 1784. Returning to Anne Arundel County, Weems served in small parishes for eight or nine years with zeal and industry—and with the joie de vivre that was so characteristic of him.

He often shocked his fellow preachers. On one such occasion, he wrote and peddled a pamphlet entitled *Onania* at a church convention. He once praised Tom Paine's *Age of Reason* from the pulpit in a Virginia diocese, and when Bishop Meade of Virginia remonstrated, Weems noted that he sold the antidote with the bane, offering bishop and parishioners alike a choice of Paine's book or the book by the Bishop of Llandaff, who rebuked Paine. Even while preaching, Weems sold a few books on the side.

It was not long before Weems' innate urge to wander got the better of him. Gathering some books and a few tracts that he himself had written, Weems abandoned rural Maryland and became an itinerant bookseller.

In a short time the Episcopal rector—he of high spirits and merry countenance—joined forces with the solid man-of-business and Roman Catholic, Mathew Carey. This was in 1793, and these two unlike personalities were to be joined together for approximately a third of a century, marred only by two brief infidelities on Weems' part. One of these came about in 1802 when Weems hitched his cart to that of Caleb P. Wayne of Philadelphia, who was publishing Chief Justice Marshall's *Life of Washington*, a multivolume set. Unfortunately, the distinguished justice was prolix, and the first volume published was much larger than Wayne expected; thereupon, the publisher cut Weems' commission and cheapened the binding in an effort to recoup his investment. While the loss of commission was a sad blow to Weems, he reacted even more strongly to the cheapened binding and wrote an angry letter to Wayne. Throughout his life, Weems insisted on quality bindings, maintaining that books with poor bindings were hard to sell.[1] While working for Wayne the wily parson made an arrangement on the side with Mathew Carey. Carey provided Weems with a light carriage and a salary of $1,250 per year.[2]

Soon the parson became a familiar figure to travelers through the south and mid-Atlantic states. Described by William Gilmore Simms as "with cheerful bright, mercurial eye and of a laughing, sunshiny countenance, the expression of which was merry," he could be seen bouncing along the wretched roads in his two-horse carriage filled with books and his ever-present fiddle by his side.

Mason Weems often "set up" in the town squares, standing on his wagon to hawk his books. He was never loath to pursue his customers into taverns and often pretended to be boozy and cup-stricken. When he gained the attention of the local tipplers, he would deliver a sermon on drink, produce his

Two Hundredth Anniversary

pamphlets and books, and seldom fail to have excellent returns. He played his fiddle at fairs and weddings, delivered impromptu sermons at local churches upon request, and generally managed to tie in a commercial message about one of Carey's publications or one of his own.

Weems wrote a number of books and pamphlets in addition to his bestselling *Life of Washington*, which reached 70 editions, plus some pirated ones. One of his most interesting biographies was the *Life of General Francis Marion*,[3] co-authored by Peter Horry, a lieutenant in Marion's command. Horry was appalled by the liberties that he accused Weems of taking in the telling of the story. Though Weems made a few changes in subsequent editions, he was apparently undisturbed by the controversy. As noted before, he was accustomed to controversy, having long carried on a correspondence of unparalleled virulence with his employer, Carey. Weems complained about ill-treatment, hardships on the road, commissions, deliveries, and, of course, Carey's bindings.[4] In 1825 he died in harness in Beaumont, South Carolina.[5] His remains were taken home to his loving and much-loved wife, Fanny, about whom Weems once wrote the following delightful verse:

> While some for pleasure pawn their health,
> 'Twixt Lais and the Bagni-O
> I'll save myself and without stealth
> Kiss and caress my Fanny-O
> She bids more fair t'engage a Jove
> Than Leda did or Danae-O
> Were I to paint the queen of love
> None else should sit but Fanny-O. . . . [6]

Taking off on this, Morris Bishop, writing in the *New Yorker Magazine* in 1936, suggested this epitaph for Parson Weems' grave:

> With moral tales & Bible sales
> He gained an earthly glory-O
> And now he meets in Salem's streets
> His finest territory-O.

NOTES

1. Weems talked Carey into publishing an expensive red morocco-bound edition of the Bible, which largely through Weems' efforts sold very well.

2. Weems' salary was $470 more than that which Christian C. Febiger Spahr, partner, received from Carey's descendants when he joined the firm in 1935.

3. In Weems' book, *Life of General Francis Marion,* he describes a raid by Marion's soldiers on a British camp. Taken by surprise the British soldiers were sitting about drinking and gaming when Marion appeared. Weems' wrote: "One of the gamblers, though shot dead, still held the cards gripped in his hands. Led by curiosity to inspect this strange sight, a dead gambler, we found that the cards which he held were ace, deuce and jack. Clubs were trumps. Holding high, low, jack and the game in his own hand, he seemed to be in a fair way to do well, but Marion came down upon him with a trump that spoiled his sport and non-suited him forever."

4. Here is a sampling of that correspondence: *Carey to Weems (February 10, 1807):* "My connection with you has been from its earliest contract a source of chagrin, vexation and loss." *Weems to Carey (August 10, 1810):* "Why in God's name won't you put as I ten thousand times begged you the catalogues in my box? Nothing will ever be done as it ought—you want money; then, why say I grumble because I asked you for books which will bring you money." *Weems to Carey (March 31, 1814):* "Nothing

Dumfries, August 1, 1818.

M. L. WEEMS

RESPECTFULLY SOLICITS THE SUBSCRIPTIONS OF HIS FRIENDS, FOR

Armstrong's Edition of

Scott's Family Bible,

IN SIX VOLUMES OCTAVO.

TERMS OF PUBLISHING.

I. It shall be printed on good white paper, and with a fair type.

II. It will be comprised in SIX LARGE VOLUMES, containing the Old and New Testaments, with the Introductory Observations to the Books, &c. and the NOTES and PRACTICAL OBSERVATIONS. The marginal references, which by the generality of readers are never used, will be omitted, and thereby room will be made to put the Notes and Practical Observations in a LARGER TYPE, for the accommodation of all readers, but particularly the *aged ;* thus uniting PORTABLE VOLUMES with a GOOD FAIR type, and making these editions, for common use, the BEST AND CHEAPEST EDITIONS EVER PUBLISHED.

III. Price to subscribers, twenty-one dollars, bound—to non-subscribers, twenty-four.

EXTRACTS OF LETTERS TO THE PUBLISHER.

From the Rev. Dr. Griffin.—" I esteem Dr. Scott's Family Bible eminently calculated to promote the cause of truth and piety. It seems scarcely possible for one to read daily the Notes and Observations in the Family Bible, without becoming a wiser and better man."

Rev. Asa Eaton, of Boston.—" I am happy to learn that you are about giving to the public another edition of Scott's Family Bible. It is a TREASURE WHICH EVERY FAMILY OUGHT TO POSSESS. For the success of your undertaking you have my best wishes and fervent prayers."

Rev. Daniel Sharp, of Boston.—" Dear Sir, The name of Scott is so well known, and his character as an author so firmly established, and so justly admired in the religious world, that a recommendation of his Family Bible appears almost superfluous. The more it is read by pious Christians, the more extensive will be its circulation."

Rev. Dr. Holmes, of Cambridge.—" Dear Sir, I believe Scott's Family Bible peculiarly suitable for the use of families and private Christians, as being eminently adapted to advance the knowledge of the Holy Scriptures, and in harmony with *their* grand design, to make men " wise to salvation, through faith which is in Christ Jesus."

Rev. Dr. Baldwin, of Boston.—" I feel free to say, that in my estimation Scott's Family Bible deservedly ranks among our ablest and best commentaries. All the leading doctrines of Christianity, as professed and maintained by many of the most eminent reformers, are in my judgment very happily illustrated and enforced."

Rev. James Winchell, of Boston.—" I cordially unite in the above recommendations."

From the Rev. Dr. Dana, of Newburyport.—" Dr. Scott's Commentary has merited and obtained a distinguished popularity. His " Practical Observations" constitute a fund of rich, diversified, and impressive instruction. Even a few of them read to a family in the morning, cannot fail to furnish its members with materials for profitable r-flection through the day. The style is judicious and happy ; being neither above the ignorant, nor below the learned. It is uniformly perspicuous, pure, and energetic ; and sometimes, with its subject, rises into sublimity. Above all, the *spirit* which pervades the work is excellent. It is the meek, affectionate, healing, yet faithful spirit of the Gospel."

Rev. Dr. Morse, of Charlestown.—" Dear Sir, The character of Dr. Scott's Commentary on the Bible is so generally known and so highly approved, that I deem further recommendations needless. This most excellent and useful work I ardently wish was in every family in the United States."

Rev. Dr. Sanders, of Medfield.—" Sincere inquirers into a knowledge of duty will always rise from a perusal of its pages with minds more enlightened, with good resolutions strengthened, and with the best affections invigorated. The Practical Observations are particularly valuable, and give to this work its most distinguishing excellence."

Rev. Joshua Bates, of Dedham.—" Sir, I am pleased with your proposals for publishing Scott's Family Bible, and sincerely wish you success in the undertaking. I am acquainted with no commentary on the Sacred Scriptures, which I would more cordially recommend for general use. If you execute the work with your usual fidelity and care, I have no doubt that it will be well patronized by the religious public."

Rev. Joshua Huntington, of Boston.—" Perhaps in no way can ministers, instructors of youth, and private Christians, do greater service to society, than by exerting themselves to disseminate this truly invaluable work."

Commendations, equally cordial, have been bestowed on SCOTT'S FAMILY BIBLE, by reverend gentlemen of *different religious denominations,* among whom are,

Rev. *Ashbel Green, Princeton College.*
Rev. *Samuel S. Smith,* Do.
Rev. *William Rodgers, Philadelphia,* and
Rev. *Joseph Emerson, Beverly,* with the words of which latter divine, we conclude :

" Six editions of this great work (Scott's Family Bible) have been published in this country.

" I have had considerable opportunity to examine and compare specimens of all these six editions, and am decidedly of opinion, that most people would greatly prefer ARMSTRONG'S EDITION, now publishing in Boston. It has the advantage of being cheaper, less cumbersome, and more elegant.

" ARMSTRONG'S EDITION, therefore, is the one which I can most highly recommend for the use of families. It is peculiarly calculated to supersede the use of a large Bible ; and in two respects it will answer a better purpose, merely for reading the Scriptures; as it is less cumbersome, and may be read by several persons at the same time."

SUBSCRIBERS' NAMES.	RESIDENCE.	NO. OF COPIES.

An advertising piece used by Weems

so grieves and surprises me as your letters. I never read them without exclaiming My God! What a pity that a gentleman of so many amiable, so many divine qualities should yield to an irritability that not only obscurates the finest mind but betrays the best heart into acts of such violence and impatience.
You brand me as a perfect Monster for just asking you to let me have old books at a discount of 40 when I can get branding new and better sorts at 45."

5. A curious tale was related by Davy Crockett in his supposed autobiography published by Mathew Carey's son, Edward, partner in the firm of Carey & Hart. Crockett claims that a man dressed in black, of merry countenance, selling books from his wagon and playing on his fiddle, appeared at a tavern where Crockett was staying. Crockett places the time of this occurrence long after Weems' death. Crockett doesn't say what he was drinking when the apparition appeared.

6. Lais was a celebrated Greek courtesan and a Bagni-O is a brothel. Danae, mother of Perseus, was locked in a tower but nonetheless managed to become impregnated by Zeus, who changed himself into a shower of gold.

Two Hundredth Anniversary

29

Henry C. Carey

Henry C. Carey, "The Bookseller in Miniature," and His Partner, Isaac Lea

III

Sad though it be, the abilities and energies of fathers are sometimes not visited on sons. Such was not the case, however, with Mathew Carey's eldest son, Henry C. Carey (born December 15, 1793), who like his father had a sketchy education but a passion for reading. Mathew furthered his son's education by taking Henry, while still a young child, on long walks through Philadelphia, in the course of which the elder Carey pointed out good business practices and lectured on economic principles.

These walks may have contributed to Henry's precocity, for at the age of nine he journeyed to New York with a stock of books and conducted business at a book fair that his father had set up. The Philadelphia press was intrigued by this and dubbed young Carey "The Bookseller in Miniature." He did well enough in New York that his father sent him to Baltimore, where for six months Henry, at the tender age of 11, managed the Baltimore branch of his father's store.

Increasingly active in the business, Henry was made a partner on January 1, 1817, at the age of 23. Henry C. Carey took full control of the firm in 1822 and then accepted a partner, Isaac Lea, who had married his sister, Frances Anne Carey.

Isaac Lea, born in 1792, was an interesting man in his own right and made a good business companion to Carey. John Tebbel, the publishing historian, states that "Carey was the imaginative one and Isaac the steady plugger. Isaac was retiring and Henry assertive." On the other hand, Lea was described by a contemporary as "self-confident and strong-willed."[1] Whatever Lea's personality may have been, he led an active social life, wrote 279 scientific papers, mostly in malacology (the study of mollusks), became the President of the American Association for the Advancement of Science and the President of the Academy of Natural Sciences of Philadelphia, as well as the Vice President of the American Philosophical Society. While achieving the foregoing, he and his wife brought into the world two sons and one daughter.[2] Lea retired in 1851, but lived on to the great age of 95; he died on December 8, 1886, leaving behind his great collections of shells and minerals and an important collection of Italian art.

Carey, our "bookseller in miniature," was a dynamic man. In 1820 he and his father launched *The Philadelphia Journal of the Medical and Physical Sciences*, edited by Nathaniel Chapman, which in 1828 became *The American Journal of the Medical Sciences*. This publication remained with the company until 1969, when it was sold. In 1822 he opened a New York branch of the firm which, in

Nathaniel Chapman

Isaac Lea's house at 1622 Locust Street, built in 1851

addition to selling books, also published ten titles under the imprint H. C. Carey & Co. The New York firm suffered various misfortunes, including a burglary, and Carey shut it down a year after it opened.

By 1826 Henry Carey had brought into his catalog two of the most widely read and highly respected American authors, Washington Irving and James Fenimore Cooper, whose first novels were published by Wiley of New York. David Kaser, who wrote about the firm, relates that, "It would appear that the Carey firms were among the first to patronize to any great extent American authors and to pay them well for their works." In an effort to develop more native American talent, Carey launched two magazines, the *Atlantic Souvenir* (1825) and the *American Quarterly Review* (1827). Neither lasted long, a fate that befell many magazines in those days. He also published *El Aguinaldo*, a Spanish literary manual, which appeared to be successful but nonetheless vanished shortly.

Though his list was small, it was carefully selected by Henry C. Carey himself and was highly profitable. In 1822 he published 42 books, followed by 28 in 1823, and 37 in 1824. The year 1822 was particularly profitable, for Carey published Scott's *Life of Napoleon Buonaparte* in an edition of 12,250 copies. Despite the fact that Carey paid Scott $1,475 for the work at a time when many foreign writers received nothing, and sank $20,000 into production, he made a tidy profit of $13,000 on that title alone. In 1829 he brought out the first of a 13-volume work, translated from German, under the title,

Two Hundredth Anniversary

James Fenimore Cooper

Encyclopedia Americana. He paid the translation staff $20,000 for their efforts. The range and variety of Carey's publications, and those who followed him, are displayed in *The Cost Book of Carey & Lea, 1825–1838*, edited by David Kaser.[3]

Dickens' *Posthumous Papers of the Pickwick Club* was published in November, 1836, in an edition of 1500 copies by Carey, Lea & Blanchard. The entire cost of composition, press work, and paper was $207.26. "Doing up," the quaint word for binding used in the cost book, was 7 cents. The unit cost of 1500 bound copies was 21 cents. The selling price of the book is not given, but in the later years of the nineteenth century the firm normally set the list price at 3.3 times the manufacturing cost. Dickens published six other books with the firm, including *Oliver Twist.*

The American Cyclopedia of Practical Medicine and Surgery, by the distinguished physician, Isaac Hays, was published in two volumes in 1834 and 1836. In 1834, 750 copies of the *Posthumous Poems of the Reverend George Crabbe* were published; it would be interesting to know how well that particular work sold. In 1835, the *Journal* of Fanny Kemble,[4] the famous British actress who married a Philadelphian after an American tour, was published in an edition of 8000 copies, four times the number of copies printed for the book, *Lafayette in America in 1824 and 1825*, which the firm published in 1829.

Benjamin Disraeli's popular novel *Vivian Grey* was published in 1827, the very year that the firm brought out a book on prison discipline. In 1833 the firm published the *Select Works* of Tobias Smollett.

Charles Dickens

Fanny Kemble

The firm published many women writers. Frances Kemble has already been mentioned, but there was a host of others, the best known being Jane Austen and Mary Shelley, whose *Frankenstein* was published in 1833. In 1842 Lea and Blanchard published *The Works of Mrs. Hemans*, the Victorian poetess, in a seven-volume set.

In April, 1827, the company went through yet another name change. The occasion was the bringing into partnership of Henry's younger brother, Edward L. Carey. The imprint became Carey, Lea & Carey, with Henry owning half of the business and Isaac and Edward dividing the remainder. Two years after Edward joined the firm, and despite its profitability, he decided to ally himself with Abraham Hart, a Philadelphia stationer, and to assume the firm's retail book operations, remaining in the same building on the corner of Fourth and Chestnut. Henry and Isaac retained the publishing and wholesale ends of the business and reorganized themselves, once again, as Carey and Lea.[5]

In 1833, the oft-changed imprint became Carey, Lea & Blanchard when William A. Blanchard, who had worked for the firm since 1812, became a partner. There is little to be found about Blanchard and his influence on the firm. Tebbel describes him as a "faithful and unobtrusive employee" who remained that way after becoming a partner. He presumably took no creative role in publishing policy, but gave Carey and Lea more time to pursue their outside writing interests. Another employee of the firm was Presley Blakiston, who came to Carey and Lea in 1826, where he remained for 17 years, leaving in

1843 to form a partnership with Robert Lindsay. Blakiston's firm became a leading and highly respected medical publisher, which was first bought by Doubleday and then in 1954 by McGraw-Hill.

In the decade of the 1830s, the firm found itself locked in a competitive battle with the Harper Brothers—James, John, Wesley, and Fletcher—whose establishment rose quickly from a modest beginning in 1817 to become a major American publishing house. The battle revolved primarily around the reprint rights for British works and the goal was supremacy in American publishing. International copyright law, which the Harpers actively opposed, did not exist, and the two firms found themselves striving to get out the latest novel from England before the competition did. In the case of the third volume of Scott's *Peveril of the Peak*, the Harpers managed to secure the book from the ship before it docked, and by round-the-clock labor, the finished book appeared in the bookstores long before Carey's edition, which was being set from proofs purchased in advance in London. The cost of such competition proved unprofitable for both firms, and Fletcher Harper and Henry Carey, after extensive correspondence, agreed on the "Harper rule." According to this agreement, prior claim to publication was established by a firm's publicly announcing its intention to reprint. The rule operated by courtesy of the trade and was to be enforced by "reprisals against trespassers," in Fletcher's words. The Harper rule worked well enough, although the firms never did agree on a definition of "reprisals against trespassers," nor on the issue of a publisher's exclusive rights to the works of a particular author. Carey's retirement in

Two Hundredth Anniversary

41

1838 ended the feud; his remaining partners, Blanchard and Lea, seemed to lose their zest to do battle with the Harpers for the British imports, and gradually turned more and more to the publication of medical and scientific literature, a field in which they already had an attractive and growing list.[6]

The movement toward scientific publishing was also hastened by the extreme business depression between 1839 and 1843, which rendered general literature less attractive. Large stocks of Cooper's novels bound in cloth were utterly unsalable and had to be stripped of their covers and done up in paper to find a market. General publishing began to center more and more in New York.

Though Carey had retired (and the firm once again changed its name—this time to Lea & Blanchard), he remained active, writing a number of books on political economy. His major work, *Principles of Political Economy,* appeared in three volumes in 1837, 1838, and 1840 and enjoyed an enormous vogue in Europe. Carey's books were translated into French, German, Italian, Swedish, Russian, Hungarian, Portuguese, and Japanese. His political beliefs tended to favor a laissez-faire approach to trade until the passage of the Tariff Act of 1842, which went against his interests. Finally, in 1848, having been previously unable to reconcile protectionism with any economic theory, he suddenly saw the light, and as he reported, "jumped out of bed, and dressed, and was a Protectionist from that hour." His crusade to protect American industry from foreign goods went on for 30 years and resulted in a remarkable outpouring of magazines, pamphlets, and books, which won him a national reputation. This culminated in the publication of *Principles of Social Science*, which he thought to be his greatest work, published between 1858 and 1860.

Henry C. Carey was an attractive man, described by contemporaries as 5 feet, 10 inches tall, weighing about 160 pounds, "a black-eyed, white-haired man with a very piercing glance." He radiated warmth and urgency and enjoyed drama, opera, and the literary world. He was widely respected and was asked to run for governor of New Jersey, where he lived for a time, as well as for governor of Pennsylvania. He was even sounded out for the Presidency, but he had little interest in political office. An English writer, Leslie, noted that Carey was addicted to profanity and "swore like a bargeman." A biographer, Green, stated that he was contentious like his father, impetuous, hard driving, and an "addict of the grape." Though democratic by nature, he was curiously fond of a most undemocratic Czar and of Napoleon III. His attitude toward slavery and the Southern secession was "a plague on both your houses."

Two Hundredth Anniversary

Like his father he was many-sided. He was, among other things, a vice president of a local horticultural society. He worked hard raising money for an impoverished President Jefferson, for Robert Fulton, and for destitute officers of the American Revolution. Through his efforts, $25,000 in goods were sent to the Greeks in their war for independence against Turkey (1821–1829), and he presided at the "Carey Vespers," a weekly meeting of prominent citizens where, as Carey wrote, "We discuss everything and decide nothing."

His influence on political and economic affairs was enormous in his time. His impact on publishing may be summed up by a figure quoted in Tebbel's *History of Book Publishing in the United States:* when Carey became a partner in 1822, the market value of all books published in Philadelphia was $110,000. In 1830 Carey & Lea alone published books with a market value of more than $150,000.

Two Hundredth Anniversary

Henry C. Carey died on October 13, 1879; his wife had died years earlier.

NOTES

1. Lea was strong-willed enough to volunteer to bear arms against the British in the War of 1812. As a consequence he was read out of the Society of Friends.

2. Isaac Lea's son, Mathew, became a chemist of note. The second son, Henry Charles Lea, was a renaissance man whose business and scholarly pursuits will be covered in Chapter 5. The daughter, Hannah Lea, is chiefly remembered for having married Christian Carson Febiger in 1817. Isaac Lea and Frances Carey Lea were also responsible for bringing up four orphaned children of relatives.

3. A cost book was a ledger in which the publisher recorded relevant information about his publications. Here, for example, is information on Victor Hugo's *Hunchback of Notre-Dame* as it appeared in Carey, Lea & Blanchard's cost book:

HUNCHBACK OF NOTRE DAME

Comp. @ .33 1/3	$173.65
Press 76 tokens @ .66 2/3	50.67
Boxes	4.00
Freight	6.00
42 reams @ 2.75	115.50
	$349.82

1000 copies cost $.35 ea. in sheets November 5, 1834

Hugo, Victor Marie, *comte*. The hunchback of Notre-Dame. With a sketch of the life and writings of the author; by Frederick Shoberl. Philadelphia: Carey, Lea and Blanchard. 1834.

Cost books from 1800–1811 and 1825–1909 are at The Historical Society of Pennsylvania. Lea & Febiger continues to keep a cost book, the facts being carefully hand-written as always.

4. Fanny (Frances Anne) Kemble, 1809–1893, made her acting debut as Juliet in 1829 in Covent Garden. Her acting ability received extravagent praise in the course of an American tour in 1832. In 1834 she married Pierce Butler of Philadelphia and went with him to his Georgia estate. Her revulsion to slavery was expressed in another publication, put out by Longman, called *Journal of a Residence on a Georgia Plantation in 1838–1839*. She divorced Butler, returned to England, and continued to write against slavery. Her journal and *Records of a Later Life* are useful sourcebooks.

Two Hundredth Anniversary

5. Many people thought that the firms of Carey & Lea and Carey & Hart were rivals, but actually they worked closely together. Edward Carey, who was enterprising, had a great success with the *Life of David Crockett*. He also published Longfellow's poetry and some popular British novels. Carey died in 1845, and Hart continued the business with the help of Carey's nephew, Henry Carey Baird. Hart retired in 1854 and the printing plates were sold at auction for unprecedented prices. The books were sold to a bookseller, Parry and MacMillan.

6. Tebbel tells a story about the Harper firm that is apropos to absolutely nothing, but is too delightful to skip over. In 1833 the firm installed a steam press, and the horse that had walked for years in circles around a horsepower press was shipped to the Harpers' Long Island farm for a well-earned retirement. The horse spent the rest of its life walking around a tree in the pasture from seven in the morning until six at night, its usual working hours. When the noon whistle blew at a neighboring factory, it took its customary lunch hour.

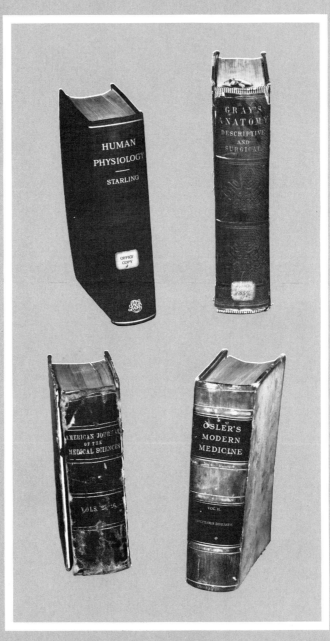

Earlier titles by Lea & Febiger and predecessor firms

Nineteenth Century American Medical Literature: A Gallery of Lea Titles
Francesco Cordasco

IV

1

When Austin Flint, Professor of Medicine, Bellevue Hospital Medical College, completed the fifth edition of his *Treatise on the Principles and Practice of Medicine* (1884), he wrote in its Preface: "The author . . . tenders his thanks to the present publishers for a continuance of the courtesy and kindness which rendered most agreeable his relations, for a quarter of a century, with their predecessors, Blanchard & Lea, and Henry C. Lea."

The sentiments were reaffirmed in the Preface to the sixth edition of the *Principles and Practice* (1886) by Austin Flint, *fils*, himself a distinguished clinician.[1] The long life of the *Principles and Practice*, whose first edition had appeared in 1866, ended with its seventh edition in 1894. These editions chronicled the evolution of modern clinical medicine over the course of the latter part of the nineteenth century. Austin Flint, *fils*, noted that his father's text derived from "an unbroken series of records of cases in private practice and in

Austin Flint

hospitals, begun in 1833 and continued for more than half a century, covering sixteen thousand nine hundred and twenty-two folio pages of manuscript, written with the author's own hand." Austin Flint's *Principles and Practice* epitomized the history and development of an indigenous American medical literature, a history in which the descendants of Mathew Carey played an important part.

The eminent nineteenth century surgeon, Samuel D. Gross, was keenly aware of the importance of Mathew Carey and his descendants. In an introductory address to the Fifty-First Course of Lectures in the Jefferson Medical College in 1875, Gross sketched *The History of American Medical Literature from 1776 to the Present Time:*

"The great publishing house, however, of the country was that originally of the Careys, descendants of Mathew Carey, an Irish gentleman of great intelligence and enterprise, who was himself engaged in the book business from 1785 till 1822. He then formed a partnership with his sons, which expired in 1825, when Carey, Lea & Carey came upon the stage, then Carey & Lea; Carey, Lea & Blanchard; Lea & Blanchard; and Blanchard & Lea, who, after a reign of fourteen years, were succeeded by Mr. Henry C. Lea, the eminent medical book publisher, who has ever since been his own master. From these respective firms a large majority of our native and reprinted medical works have emanated, and it affords me pleasure to add that they all have been fully rewarded for their labor and the investment of their capital."

(A listing of the various firm names with their dates appears on the endpapers).

Henry C. Lea, who published Gross's long essay for distribution among Gross's "professional brethren" in 1876, was clearly unashamed of the essay's historical judgments. And Gross's judgment was reaffirmed a near-century later by the historian of American book publishing, John Tebbel, who in his *History of Book Publishing in the United States*, stated flatly: "By 1875, Lea had made his firm the largest publisher of medical, surgical and scientific books in the world, and in addition published four important medical periodicals."

Two Hundredth Anniversary

Writing in *A Century of American Medicine, 1776–1876*,[2] John S. Billings, the creator of the Surgeon General's Library and the architect of its *Index Catalogue*, surveyed the state of American medical publishing. Billings made use of "statistics obtained from a nearly complete list of the medical books published in this country from 1776 to the present," and from which "it may be considered certain that no important work has been omitted." The books that he counted were classified as follows: I. Systematic treatises and monographs by physicians residing in this country, including reports of hospitals, corporations, and government departments; II. Reprints and translations of foreign medical books; III. Medical journals; IV. Transactions of medical societies. Classes I, III, and IV include what Billings regarded as American medical literature, and he illustrated his findings with a carefully designed table, of which we have provided a facsimile reproduction at the top of the opposite page.

Billings subjected his statistics to careful analysis, primarily seeking answers to two questions: Where

Table showing number of *Medical Books* printed in the United States from January 1, 1776, to January 1, 1876.

		1775 to 1799	1800 to 1809	1810 to 1819	1820 to 1829	1830 to 1839	1840 to 1849	1850 to 1859	1860 to 1869	1870 to 1875	Total.
CLASS I. American Medical Books	No. 1st edition	39	24	51	48	83	96	101	157	130	729
	No. later editions	9	4	14	17	34	49	80	85	44	336
	No. Vols. Total	51	31	77	86	136	162	197	256	180	1176
CLASS II. Reprints and Trans.	No. 1st edition	28	39	64	72	145	135	99	104	81	767
	No. later editions	11	23	28	33	36	67	76	64	50	388
	No. Vols. Total	49	76	111	135	192	214	184	160	137	1274
CLASS III. Medical Journals	No. Journs.com'ced	1	5	6	17	18	26	52	38	32	195
	" " discont'd	......	3	5	10	18	14	31	36	20	137
"A." Original	No. Vols. com'nced	2	21	27	85	104	173	376	292	296	1376
	No. Vols. compl'ted	2	20	27	79	98	166	366	271	283	1312
"B." Reprints	No. Journals	......	......	1	4	......	.5	1	3	3	17
	No. Volumes	......	......	9	29	20	46	71	51	32	258
CLASS IV. Transactions Med. Societies	No. Volumes	7	3	2	5	17	27	76	88	111	336

Two Hundredth Anniversary

(Reproduced from Billings: *A Century of American Medicine.*)

had the works been published? By whom had they been published? His findings surely were not unanticipated. Philadelphia was the acknowledged center of medical publishing, and the Lea imprint was the dominating presence: "It appears . . . that more than one-half of our medical books have been published in Philadelphia, and about one-fifth in New York. The firm of Carey, Lea & Carey, now H. C. Lea, has published nearly six hundred editions of medical works; and those of Lindsay & Blakiston, and Lippincott, each between one and two hundred. In New York, the principal publishing house is that of S. S. & W. Wood, now Wm. Wood & Co., which has issued about one hundred and fifty

(150) editions." Six hundred titles! The ubiquity of the Lea imprint helps explain Professor Gross's earlier observation and its reaffirmation by John Tebbel a century later. The Carey descendants had, indeed, become "the largest publisher of medical, surgical and scientific books in the world."

A selection of titles out of this overwhelming Lea presence is a difficult task, made somewhat easier if the criteria of selection use as a guide works of the stature of Austin Flint's *Principles and Practice of Medicine,* whose importance was attested by revision, reissue, and the acclaim of continuing use. But even with this delimitation, only a handful of works can be noted here in a few broadly representative fields: surgery; the practice of medicine; and obstetrics and gynecology.

2

Surgery

Among American portraits, the "Gross Clinic," which Thomas Eakins was commissioned to paint for the 1876 Centennial celebration, is one of the most famous for both technique and design. It depicts Dr. Gross pausing in the midst of a surgical lecture, and its visual impact gives full meaning to his eminence as a surgeon. Similarly, in the annals of surgical literature, the historical importance of Samuel D. Gross's *System of Surgery* (1859) is unchallenged. Garrison, in his book, *A Medical Bibliography: An Annotated Check-List of Texts Illustrating the History of Medicine* (Philadelphia, J. B. Lippincott Co., 1970), called it the most important surgical treatise of its time. Its last (sixth) edition appeared in 1882.

In his *Autobiography* (1887) Gross recaptured its genesis and initial appearance:

"I had commenced the composition of my Surgery several years before I left Kentucky, and I now set vigorously to work to complete it. I had sketched the plan and adopted a title, both of which met with the approval of Messrs. Blanchard & Lea, who had agreed to publish it. . . . I generally spent from five to eight hours a day upon my manuscript, subject of course to frequent and sometimes annoying interruptions by patients. In the winter I commonly sat up till eleven and half past eleven o'clock at night. I then closed my study, and almost invariably took a walk down Chestnut Street as far as the State House, in order to obtain a little fresh air and to shake off my mind the subject upon which I had been so assiduously engaged. By this means I generally succeeded in obtaining a good night's rest with sound and refreshing sleep. Unless I was greatly interrupted, I seldom wrote less than from ten to fifteen pages of foolscap in the twenty-four hours, and I rarely retired until they were carefully corrected. It was not often I rewrote anything, although I not unfrequently interlined. In the winter, during the continuance of the lectures, my pen was less active than in the recess, but I nevertheless seldom failed to do a good day's work. I jogged along in this manner until early in the spring of 1859, when, the manuscript being ready, the printers commenced their task, and I the hard one of proof-reading. The preface was dated July 8th, 1859. Soon after, the work was issued in two portly octavo volumes, numbering, in the aggregate, two thousand three hundred and sixty pages, and profusely illustrated by engravings on wood. The mechanical execution was highly creditable to the publishers, printers, and artists. The edition comprised two thousand copies, and cost a large sum of money, enough, as Blanchard & Lea assured me, to have enabled them to open a respectable mercantile house on Market Street."

Two Hundredth Anniversary

Samuel D. Gross published considerably more under the Lea imprints. His *Elements of Pathological Anatomy* (1836) appeared in a third revised edition in 1857; Garrison called it "the first exhaustive study in English of the subject." The first edition of his *Practical Treatise on the Diseases, Injuries and Malformations of the Urinary Bladder, the Prostate Gland, and the Urethra* was published in 1851, and his *Practical Treatise on Foreign Bodies in the Air Passages* appeared in 1854, "the first systematic study of the subject" (Garrison). The elder Gross was joined by his son, Samuel Weissel Gross, as a Lea author, and he published *A Practical Treatise on Impotence, Sterility and Allied Disorders of the Male Sexual Organs* (1881), which went through four editions, the last appearing in 1890. S. W. Gross also assisted his father in the later editions of his great *System of Surgery*.

Two Hundredth Anniversary

A vast number of works in surgical literature appeared under the Lea imprints of the nineteenth century, ranging from the works of English surgeons published in the early century to the great multivolumed "systems" published toward the century's close. The *Principles of Surgery* (1845) and the *Practice of Surgery* (1846) of James Miller are representative of the early English works, and these are joined by the still earlier *Institutes and Practice of Surgery* (1827) of William Gibson and the *Principles and Practice of Surgery* (1825) of Sir Astley Paston Cooper.

The early English authors are the precursors of a continuing appearance under the Lea imprints of English and Scots physicians. Even with the emergence of a strong indigenous American medical literature by mid-century, the English connection was not abandoned. Joining S. D. Gross's *System of Surgery* (1859) in the mid-century are the Scots surgeon, William Pirrie, *Principles and Practice of Surgery* (1852), and the London surgeons, Robert Druitt, *Principles and Practice of Modern Surgery* (1852), Frederick Carpenter Skey, *Operative Surgery* (1851), and John Eric Erichsen, *The Science and Art of Surgery* (1854), "the most popular text-book on the subject for many years" (Garrison).

In a class by itself is the work of the well known London anatomist, Joseph Maclise, whose *Surgical Anatomy,* in "large imperial quarto, with 68 large and splendid plates," Lea & Blanchard published in 1859. The Maclise volume represents a supreme artistic achievement in anatomic illustration, and anticipates the work of the Johns Hopkins medical illustrator, Max Brödel.

Beyond S. D. Gross, the major American surgeons in the Lea canons include John Ashhurst, whose *Principles and Practice of Surgery* (1871) went through six editions, the last published in 1893; Stephen Smith, *Principles and Practice of Operative Surgery* (1887); and Lewis A. Stimson, *A Manual of Operative Surgery* (1878), whose fourth edition appeared in 1900. In the related surgical specialties, the *Practical Treatise on Fractures and Dislocations* (1860; 8th ed., 1891) of Frank Hastings Hamilton remained a leading text, asserting Hamilton's preeminence as a surgeon. Frederic S. Dennis, Professor of Surgery, Bellevue Hospital Medical School, served as general editor of the mammoth *System of Surgery,* whose four volumes appeared between 1895 and 1896. Tucked away in its first volume is an invaluable "History and Literature of Surgery," prepared by John S. Billings. A companion work was *A Treatise on Surgery by American Authors* (1896, 2 vols.; condensed edition with revisions, 1899), edited by Roswell Park, longtime Professor of Surgery at the University of Buffalo. A synthesis of American surgical technique as it evolved across the nineteenth century is available in John Bingham Roberts' book, *A Manual of Modern Surgery*, a compact volume of 800 pages (1890; 2nd ed., 1899), and in the still more concise *Surgery* (1893) of Bern Budd Gallaudet.

The adaptation of English works to the needs of American practitioners was skillfully pursued, and an excellent example was the publication of the giant *System of Surgery, Theoretical and Practical* in three volumes (1881–1882), edited by Timothy Holmes, Hunterian Professor of Surgery at the Royal College of Surgeons. This work was "thoroughly revised and much enlarged" by John H. Packard, an eminent surgeon.

One of the most prolific surgical authors of the late nineteenth century was the Englishman, Sir Frederick Treves, of "elephant-man" fame. He was an important author in the Lea lists, and among his works were *Surgical Applied Anatomy* (1883; 2nd ed., 1883; 3rd ed., 1888); *Manual of Operative Surgery* (1892); and his *Students' Handbook of Surgical Operations* (1892). Treves acquired world fame by his operation on King Edward VII for appendicitis in 1902. Lea was the American publisher of his celebrated Jacksonian Prize Essay, *Intestinal Obstruction* (1884).

The Practice of Medicine

Mention has been made of Austin Flint's *Principles and Practice of Medicine.* In a very real sense, Professor Flint was the quintessential Lea author, producing a score of works for the Lea presses. The supreme diagnostician (Samuel D. Gross: "I know of no one who is so well entitled as Austin Flint to be regarded as the American Laennec"), Flint first described the murmur present at the apex beat in aortic regurgitation (the "Austin Flint murmur"), and his *Treatise on the Diagnosis, Pathology, and Treatment of Diseases of the Heart* (1859; 2nd ed., 1870) has an important place in the annals of American cardiology. The range of Austin Flint's work in American medical practice is best suggested by the short-title subjoined list:

Two Hundredth Anniversary

Physical Exploration and Diagnosis of Diseases Affecting the Respiratory Organs (1856; 2nd ed., 1866)

Phthisis: Its Morbid Anatomy, Aetiology . . . Treatment and Physical Diagnosis (1875)

A Manual of Percussion and Auscultation . . . (1876; 5th ed., 1890)

Clinical Medicine . . . (1879)

The long and excellent relationship between Austin Flint and his publisher is attested to by Henry C. Lea's publication of Flint's *Essays on Conservative Medicine and Kindred Topics* (1874), an eloquent plea for rational therapeutics and a classic in the history of American medical practice, in which Flint cautioned his colleagues against " . . . run[ning] a risk of shortening life by adding dangers of treatment to those of disease".

Robley Dunglison

Representative of the early practices of medicine is *General Therapeutics; or Principles of Medical Practice* (1836; 6th edition, 1857) by the Englishman Robley Dunglison, whom Thomas Jefferson had summoned to the University of Virginia. Dunglison, who was to spend most of his professional career at Jefferson Medical College in Philadelphia, was a Lea stalwart, producing a variety of influential and long-lived texts. His *Human Physiology* (1832; 8th ed., 1856), in Samuel D. Gross's words, "accomplished for [physiology] in America in the nineteenth century what Albert von Haller's great work accomplished for physiology in Europe in the eighteenth." Dunglison's *Medical Lexicon: A New Dictionary of Medical Science* appeared under the Lea imprint in 1839, and its 23rd edition, edited by his son, Richard J. Dunglison, appeared in 1893. Robley Dunglison's *Practice of Medicine; or a Treatise on Special Pathology and Therapeutics* (1842; 3rd ed., 1848), which anticipates Huntington's chorea in its description of chronic hereditary chorea in adults, is the *facile princeps* of the plethora of nineteenth century American practices, affording both model and substantive form. It clearly influenced Samuel H. Dickson's *Elements of Medicine; A Compendious View of Pathology and Therapeutics* (1855; 2nd ed., 1859). Dickson was a colleague of Robley Dunglison at Jefferson Medical College.

Amid a multitude of duties, Dunglison found time to edit and revise *The Cyclopaedia of Practical Medicine* (1845), which had been jointly edited by John Forbes and Alexander Tweedie, redoubtable Scotsmen; their *Cyclopaedia* had appeared between 1832–1835. The posthumous publication of Robley

Dunglison's *Autobiographical Ana* in 1963 reveals the mutual trust and respect that characterized the relationship between Dunglison and his publishers.[3]

Two Hundredth Anniversary

Note should also be made of Dunglison's *Elements of Hygiene* (1835; 2nd ed., 1844) and his *New Remedies: The Method of Preparing and Administering Them* (1839; 7th ed., 1856), both influential works; his work titled *The Medical Student or Aids to the Study of Medicine* (1837; 2nd ed., 1844) is an early example of a genre of medical literature that has continued to the present.

Two English titles adapted to American practice proved to be highly popular. Sir Thomas Watson, Professor at King's College, London, published his lectures in 1843; Lea & Blanchard reprinted these the next year (*Lectures on the Principles and Practice of Physic*, 1844; 5th ed., 1872). The second, third, and fourth editions were revised and enlarged by the American pediatrician, D. Francis Condie, and the fifth edition was updated by the Philadelphia physician-scientist, Henry Hartshorne. Watson's *Lectures* "formed the most important treatise of medicine for a quarter-century" (Garrison). Charles J. B. Williams, first president of the [London] Pathological Society, was the author of *Principles of Medicine* (1843), which Lea & Blanchard issued "with additions and notes by Meredith Clymer" in 1844 (5th ed., 1864). Appearing somewhat later (1876) and as popular as the American editions of Watson and Williams was the *Treatise on the Theory and Practice of Medicine* by John Syer Bristowe. Henry C. Lea published the *Treatise* "with notes and additions" by James

Howell Hutchinson, sometime editor of the *Philadelphia Medical Times*, in 1877, and a seventh edition appeared in 1890.

The American counterpart to the adapted English works was represented by the work of Henry Hartshorne, who had updated Watson's *Lectures*. Hartshorne's *Essentials of the Principles and Practice of Medicine* (1867) went through five editions, the last appearing in 1881, and it was Hartshorne whom Henry C. Lea invited to superintend the American edition of J. Russell Reynolds' elaborate *System of Medicine* (1880) in three volumes. Reynolds, Professor of Medicine at University College, London, planned and edited one of the first "systems of medicine" in English; under the Lea imprint in America it proved immensely popular. The very popularity of Reynolds' *System* led to *A System of Practical Medicine by American Authors* (1885–1886, 5 vols.), a mammoth work under the general editorship of William Pepper, Provost of the University of Pennsylvania and pioneer investigator of pernicious anemia. Pepper was assisted by Louis Starr, Clinical Professor of the Diseases of Children at the University of Pennsylvania. The publisher's prospectus proudly announced:

Two Hundredth Anniversary

"In this great work American medicine is for the first time reflected by its worthiest teachers, and presented in the full development of the practical utility which is its preeminent characteristic. The most able men—from the East and the West, from the North and the South, from all the prominent centres of education, and from all the hospitals which afford special opportunities for study and practice—have united in generous rivalry to bring together this vast aggregate of specialized experience."

A successor to the Pepper work was *A System of Practical Medicine by American Authors* (1897–1898, 4 vols.), edited by Alfred L. Loomis, Professor of Medicine at New York University and an associate of Edward L. Trudeau in the battle against tuberculosis. Loomis was assisted in editing the *System* by William Gilman Thompson. The supreme achievement in the massive multivolumed "system" genre remains *Modern Medicine, Its Theory and Practice, in Original Contributions by American and Foreign Authors* (1907–1910, 7 vols.), edited by Sir William Osler, assisted by Thomas McCrae.

Two Hundredth Anniversary

Obstetrics and Gynecology

In the Preface to his book *On the Nature, Signs, and Treatment of Childbed Fevers* (1854), Charles D. Meigs, long-time Professor of Obstetrics at Jefferson Medical College, observed:

"I believe that the only American work on the subject of Obstetrics that was in existence, when I began to study Medicine, was the small duodecimo *Compendium of Midwifery* by the venerable Dr. Samuel Bard, of New York. We had, at that day, reprints of Denman's *Midwifery*, and the two volumes of Burns, edited by Dr. James, the London Practice, pirated from Dr. Clark, and a much razed copy of Baudelocque's two fine volumes. I apprehend that, at that period, few of our American practitioners possessed more obstetric works than those I have above named, and not many, all, even of these. Since that time, we have had the benefit of Dr. Dewees's contributions, and some few others of less note than his, among them my own. There is a ground, then, in this little progress, to hope that we shall gradually obtain an American medical literature on this branch, as well as in other branches of our science."

Historically, the early development of an American literature on midwifery and obstetrics (and in a related frame of reference, on pediatrics) can be traced in the work of Charles D. Meigs and William Potts Dewees. Dewees, whose *Treatise on the Physical and Medical Treatment of Children* (1825; 11th ed., 1858) was the first American textbook on pediatrics, more than any other shaped the character of early American obstetric practice. His *Compendious System of Midwifery* (1824; 12th ed., 1852) was preceded by tentative enquiries in *Essays on Various Subjects Connected with Midwifery* (1823), and dimensionally expanded in his *Treatise on the Diseases of Females* (1826; 11th ed., 1860). Of Dewees, Samuel D. Gross wrote: "As an obstetric practitioner Dewees was one of the most popular men of his day. No woman of any social position in Philadelphia considered herself safe if she could not have Dewees in her confinement."

Two Hundredth Anniversary

Charles D. Meigs, who according to Garrison drew attention to embolism as a cause of sudden death in childbed, continued the Dewees tradition. His *Females and Their Diseases* (1848; 4th ed., 1859) was followed by his *Obstetrics: The Science and the Art* (1849; 3rd ed., 1856), and *A Treatise on Acute and Chronic Diseases of the Neck of the Uterus* (1854), which was distinguished by a set of 22 finely embellished plates. Despite his vast obstetric experience, Meigs rejected the contagion doctrine in puerperal fever. Samuel D. Gross, who knew Meigs well as a colleague at Jefferson, reminisced: "Meigs was all his life a non-believer in the infectious nature of puerperal fever, notwithstanding that for a time numerous facts demonstrative of the incorrectness of his belief

63

almost daily stared him in the face. . . . Even Professor Oliver Wendell Holmes's admirable monograph on this disease failed to convince him, and he finally died a non-contagionist."

The English tradition in obstetrics and gynecology continued in America across the nineteenth century, despite the continuing development of an American practice. The reasons are complex and related to the ease of availability of proven English works, many of which also were under the Lea imprint. Samuel Ashwell, the London obstetrician, is represented by his *Practical Treatise on the Diseases Peculiar to Women* (1845; 3rd ed., 1855), and Edward Rigby, with his *System of Midwifery* (1841; 2nd ed., 1851), exerted a wide influence. But the commanding English presence at mid-century was Fleetwood Churchill, an expatriate Englishman in practice in Dublin, where he was a Fellow of the College of Physicians. Churchill was the author of *On the Theory and Practice of Midwifery* (1843; 4th ed., 1860), which the Charleston Medical Journal called "the most popular work on midwifery ever issued from the American press." This work was paired with another book authored by Churchill, *Diseases of Females* (1843; 5th ed., 1857). Churchill's work was comprehensively augmented by his *Diseases of Infants and Children* (1850; 2nd ed., 1856) and his *Essays on Puerperal Fever* (1850). The popular *Theory and Practice of Midwifery* was "edited, with notes and additions" by D. Francis Condie, the Philadelphia pediatrician, whose own publication, *Practical Treatise on the Diseases of Children* (1844; 6th ed., 1868), was the accepted authority until superseded by the work of Meigs.

Two other English authors at mid-century deserve notice. Charles West, whose *Lectures on the Diseases of Infancy and Childhood* (1850; 5th ed., 1874) was "in its day . . . the best English work on the subject" (Garrison), was also author of *Lectures on the Diseases of Women* (1857–1858; 3rd ed., 1867), and he delivered the prestigious Croonian lectures for 1854, *An Inquiry into the Pathological Importance of Ulceration of the Os Uteri*, which Blanchard and Lea published. Francis H. Ramsbotham, obstetric physician to the London Hospital, produced *The Principles and Practice of Obstetric Medicine and Surgery* (1842; 6th ed., 1855), an imperial octavo volume, opulently illustrated with figures and lithographic plates.

Two Hundredth Anniversary

Other English authors continued the influence on American practice to the end of the nineteenth century and beyond. The more important include William Leishman, *A System of Midwifery* (1873; 4th ed., 1888); William S. Playfair, *The Science and Practice of Midwifery* (1876; 7th ed., 1898); Arthur W. Edis, *Diseases of Women* (1882); and Robert Barnes, *A System of Obstetric Medicine and Surgery* (1885).

The continuing assertion of the American practice is seen in a number of indigenous authors. Hugh Lenox Hodge, who invented the Hodge pessary, wrote *Principles and Practice of Obstetrics* in 1864 and an earlier book, *Diseases Peculiar to Women* (1860; 2nd ed., 1868). Thomas Addis Emmet, an ardent advocate of Irish home rule and an associate of J. Marion Sims at the Women's Hospital in New York City, published *Principles and Practice of Gynecology* (1879; 3rd ed., 1884). T. Gaillard Thomas, who described the first vaginal ovariotomy and

65

whose *Practical Treatise on Diseases of Women* (1868; 6th ed., 1891) was the outstanding work on the subject, was also a major figure. Thomas wrote the centennial review of American obstetrics and gynecology in *A Century of American Medicine, 1776–1876* (1876). Theophilus Parvin and Albert F. A. King deserve notice. Parvin's *The Science and Art of Obstetrics* (1886; 4th ed., 1895) proved a popular textbook, and King's *A Manual of Obstetrics* (1882; 11th ed., 1910) served as a worthy competitor. But the crowning achievements of the nineteenth century were *The American Systems of Gynecology and Obstetrics*. The *System of Gynecology by American Authors* (1887–1888, 2 vols.) was edited by Matthew D. Mann, and the *System of Obstetrics by American Authors* (1888–1889, 2 vols.) was edited by Barton Cooke Hirst. The four large octavo volumes comprised 3612 pages, with 1092 engravings and colored plates, and represented a synthesis of the medical science of the time.

3

Our self-imposed limitation to the areas of surgery, practice, and obstetrics/gynecology invites brief notice of titles in other fields. The Lea imprints covered all medical fields, and Lea catalogues (often in a 32-page signature-form appended to texts) included listings in all medical areas; the Lea Brothers & Co.'s *Classified Catalogue of Medical and Surgical Publications for 1885* adopted the following captions: Periodicals; Manuals; Dictionaries; Anatomy; Physics; Physiology; Chemistry; Pharmacy; Materia Medica; Therapeutics; Pathology; Histology; Practice of Medicine; Clinical Medicine; Hygiene; Electrical Practice; Throat,

Heart, Lungs; Nervous and Mental Diseases; Surgery; Ophthalmology; Otology; Dentistry; Urinary and Renal Diseases; Venereal Diseases; Diseases of the Skin; Diseases of Women; Midwifery; Diseases of Children; Medical Jurisprudence; Miscellaneous. This is an extraordinary coverage, itself congruent with nineteenth century optimism and encyclopedism, but still instructive to the present age. A few titles of particular significance are noted here.

Henry Gray (1827–1861) and his *Anatomy Descriptive and Surgical* (1859; 30th American ed., 1985) must be accorded a centerpiece position in nineteenth century medicine. It was originally published in London in 1858 by J. W. Parker & Son, and soon thereafter Blanchard & Lea made arrangements with Parker for its publication in the United States. It has remained a Lea publication since. Charles Mayo Goss (editor of five American editions of the *Anatomy*), in a centennial notice of the text's publication in America, observed: "We take the book for granted now, but having thrice edited it I can vouch for the enormous amount of drudgery that must have gone into the preparation of the text and the dissections which necessarily accompanied its writing. The plan of the book could not have been conceived without a phenomenal grasp of the entire subject." The first Lea editor of the *Anatomy* was Richard J. Dunglison, who had served as editor of the later editions of his father's *Medical Lexicon,* of which 23 editions occupied an illustrious place in the Lea canons. Richard Dunglison edited the first five editions of the *Anatomy* (1859, 1862, 1870, 1878, 1883); he was succeeded by the Jefferson Medical College

Henry Gray and classmates. Henry Gray appears in the foreground, second from the left

anatomist-surgeon, William W. Keen, who edited the 1887 edition. (Keen attended President Garfield in 1881 when he was shot by a disappointed office seeker.) There was no American editor for the 1893 edition. Bern Budd Gallaudet of Columbia University edited the 1896 edition. The 1905 edition was edited by J. Chalmers Da Costa of Jefferson Medical College. The *Anatomy* continued into the twentieth century edited by Edward Anthony Spitzka, Warren H. Lewis, Charles Mayo Goss and Carmine D. Clemente.

Two Hundredth
Anniversary

There were many other Lea anatomy titles, but two were of extraordinary merit. Harrison Allen, Professor of Physiology at the University of Pennsylvania (who had performed the autopsy on the celebrated Siamese twins, Chang and Eng Bunker in 1875), prepared *A System of Human Anatomy, Including Its Medical and Surgical Relations* (1884; in six sections in portfolio), which included "about 825 double-columned quarto pages, with 380 illustrations on 109 full page lithographic plates, many of which are in colors, and 241 engravings in the text." Its sumptuousness was matched by the work of John C. Dalton on *The Topographical Anatomy of the Brain* (1885) in three imperial quarto volumes "comprising about 200 pages of descriptive text . . . illustrated with forty-eight life-size photographic plates of brain sections, with a like number of outline explanatory plates, as well as many carefully-executed woodcuts through the text." Dalton, who was Professor of Physiology at Columbia University's College of Physicians and Surgeons, was the first American to devote his time exclusively to that subject, according to Garrison.

69

Outstanding publishing achievements occurred in all of the medical disciplines. In materia medica there was the *National Dispensatory* (1879; 5th ed., 1894, 1896) of Alfred Stillé and John M. Maisch, and its continuation, *The National Standard Dispensatory* (1905), edited by Hobart Amory Hare, whose *Text-Book of Practical Therapeutics* (1890; 13th ed., 1903) was the leading text of its time.

Two Hundredth Anniversary

In pathology, there is an unbroken continuity extending from the *Physiological and Pathological Anatomy* (1824) of John Davidson Godman to the *Practical Pathology* (1884) of G. Sims Woodhead. A singular event in mid-century had been the publication of the *Atlas of Pathological Histology* (1853) of Gottlieb Glüge, translated from the German by Joseph Leidy, who was an anatomist at the University of Pennsylvania and first engaged in the experimental transplantation of malignant tumors. The Glüge *Atlas* was a large imperial quarto, with 320 copper-plate figures, plain and colored, with descriptive letterpress.

Representative of dermatologic texts was that of J. Nevins Hyde, who was responsible for the naming of "prurigo nodularis" and the eponym "Hyde's disease." His book, *Practical Treatise on Diseases of the Skin* (1883; 6th ed., 1901), was joined by English works, of which the *Skin Diseases* (1880) of Malcolm Morris is typical. Central to clinical description and enquiry was the great *Atlas of Venereal Diseases* (1868) of Auguste Cullerier, which was translated with additions by Freeman J. Bumstead, whose *Pathology and Treatment of Venereal Diseases* (1861; 5th ed., 1883) continued as the standard text in the field.

In pediatrics, the development of the specialty, traditionally linked to midwifery, can be traced in the early work of D. Francis Condie, *A Practical Treatise on the Diseases of Children* (1844; 6th ed., 1868), through the continuing labors of J. Lewis Smith, whose own *Treatise on the Diseases of Infancy and Childhood* (1869; 8th ed., 1896) was the leading text for a quarter century. John M. Keating, a young and energetic nineteenth-century Dr. Benjamin Spock, prepared *The Mother's Guide in the Management and Feeding of Infants* (1881), which went through countless printings, and of which the *New York Medical Journal and Obstetrical Review* remarked in 1882: "A book small in size, written in pleasant style, in language which can be readily understood by any mother, and eminently practical and safe; in fact, a book for which we have been waiting a long time, and which we can most heartily recommend to mothers as *the* book on this subject."

Two authors, both of Philadelphia, have been left for final attention. The aristocratic, reclusive René La Roche was the antithesis of the genial and amiable novelist-physician S. Weir Mitchell. Both were Lea authors, and in their idiosyncratic differences and interests, illustrate the scope and range of the Lea influence.

René La Roche, the son of a French physician, was born in Philadelphia in 1795, took his M.D. at the University of Pennsylvania in 1820, and spent his entire professional life in the city. A founder of the Monday Evening Club (said to be the first medical club in the United States) and a member of the Philadelphia College of Physicians, he was an

Two Hundredth Anniversary

René La Roche

accomplished musician and aesthete, and one of the most erudite physicians of his time. Samuel D. Gross, who knew La Roche for many years, speaks of him affectionately:

"Dr. La Roche had an expressive and intellectual countenance, a handsome eye, and a good forehead, although his head was not very large. His highly-organized and well-balanced brain enabled him to perform a vast amount of labor. In his habits he was retiring; and he never seemed so happy as when he was in his library up to his elbow in his manuscripts. He was fond of his friends, and his friends were fond of him; and they can never forget his pleasant social visits, enlivened as they were by agreeable conversation and the recital of pertinent anecdotes, of which he had a supply of rare value. He was a charming conversationalist, always instructive, and free from affectation and pedantry. He was a great reader of light literature, was well informed respecting passing events, and could talk well upon almost any subject."

Two Hundredth Anniversary

Like most Philadelphians, La Roche was both terrified and obsessed by the "malarial fevers" out of which the dreaded yellow fever seemed to derive, and to these morbid agencies he directed most of his researches. Out of his investigations came two works: *Pneumonia: Its Supposed Connection . . . with Autumnal Fevers, Including An Inquiry into the Existence and Morbid Agency of Malaria* (1854) and his magnum opus, the 1500-page *Yellow Fever, Considered in its Historical, Pathological, Etiological, and Therapeutical Relations, Including a Sketch of the Disease as It Has Occurred in Philadelphia from 1699 to 1854* (1855, 2 vols.). More than a medical treatise, this is a kaleidoscopic social history, in which La Roche placed "before the

S. Weir Mitchell

reader an exposé of the whole subject; in a word, a comprehensive treatise on the yellow fever, in which every point of interest is fully examined." Gross testified to the work's importance:

"As a work of profound erudition, at once complete and exhaustive, written in a scholarly style, and evincing the most patient and extraordinary research, the monograph on Yellow Fever, by Dr. La Roche, is without a rival in any language. The author was at great pains and expense in obtaining everything that had been written upon the subject, and, as he himself expresses it, neglected no opportunity of rendering himself practically familiar with the disease of which he thus became the distinguished historian. The facts borrowed from the numerous writers consulted by him seem to have been verified in every instance by personal reference to their works, a task in itself of immense labor—enough, indeed, to cause the eye and brain to ache and the hand to tremble. This, assuredly, is high praise, but it is deserved. His library on yellow fever embraced the literature of all countries—the United States, Cuba, Mexico, South America, Spain, the East and West Indies, France, Germany, Italy, and Great Britain."

Two Hundredth Anniversary

It is a curious coincidence that the descendants of Mathew Carey, who had himself written a book on the yellow fever scourge in Philadelphia, were the publishers of the monumental *Yellow Fever* of René La Roche.

S. Weir Mitchell was a long-time friend and associate of Henry C. Lea; for a time he served as Lea's personal physician. The son of a noted physician (John Kearsley Mitchell), Mitchell took his M.D. at Jefferson Medical College in 1850 and devoted most of his attention to clinical neurology.

His manner of writing is engaging and easy, personal but not idiosyncratic, and unpretentious, the very opposite of René La Roche's, whose scholarship is, at times, overwhelming. These qualities may explain Mitchell's success not only as a therapist, but also as a novelist and storyteller. Mitchell inspires confidence, and the ameliorative effects of his "rest-treatment" may have well been due as much to his manner as to his prescriptive tonic remedies. For over forty years, S. Weir Mitchell was physician to the Philadelphia Orthopaedic Hospital, which under his influence became a center for the treatment of nervous disorders.

Two Hundredth Anniversary

In the Lea canons, Mitchell is represented by *Lectures on Diseases of the Nervous System, Especially in Women* (1881; 2nd ed., 1885); by *Clinical Lessons on Nervous Diseases* (1897); and by dozens of reprints extracted from the Lea medical journals and individually paginated, of which "Physiologic Studies of the Knee-Jerk, and of Reactions of Muscles under Mechanical and Other Excitants" (1886) is an example.

The *Lectures on Diseases of the Nervous System* proved more successful than most other works published under the Lea imprint in the same field, and this may also have been due to Mitchell's unpretentious and confidence-inspiring manner in a field that invited general skepticism. An excerpt from the *Lectures* illustrates Mitchell's easy manner, so compelling in its sincerity:

"What it is convenient to call the nervous temperament, or that state which may be acquired, and which I like to describe as general nervousness, is a fertile field for simulated maladies, because in it, as in hysteria, the qualities which we all possess are apt to take on a morbid development, and to get out of the limits of rational control.

"Of the individual share taken by each of these causes I shall by and by speak. Before, however, I pass on to lesser premises, I would like to digress in order to say a few words in explanation of what I mean by general nervousness. You will find this term used over and over in these lectures, and also in the annual statement of diseases treated at the Infirmary for diseases of the nervous system. I used to try to classify these cases under other heads, but came at last to see that there is a state which is best labelled thus, and that after eliminating all the cases which can be otherwise classed, a small residuum is left to which no other name applies. Some of them are more or less neurasthenic people, easily tired in brain or body; but others without this, or with this peculiarity but slightly developed, are merely tremulous nervous folks, easily agitated, over-sensitive, emotional, and timid. This state falls on man or woman or child, and is not hysteria. It is with some people a morbid birth-gift, with some an inheritance, and in its worst shapes it is made or acquired by misuse of alcohol or tobacco, or tea or coffee. Naturally you may think that such a state must be slowly created, and usually it is; but also it is true that a very permanent state of general nervousness may be evolved by the accident of a moment, when precedent conditions favor it. In a lecture on general nervousness in the male, I mentioned examples of this kind, and last week we saw at my clinic a case in which a moment of intense terror, owing to the fall of a house wall, caused in a healthy girl a state of general nervousness, alike serious and lasting. However acquired, the condition I have outlined highly favors the mimicry of disease."

The empiric soundness of Mitchell's methods is attested by modern clinicians, as quoted in *Two Centuries of American Medicine*, by James Bordley and A. McGehee Harvey, (Philadelphia: W.B. Saunders Co., 1976): "Most of his [Mitchell's] ideas arose from his clinical experience. He was one of the first American examples of the class of investigators who have the ability to weld together their laboratory observations and their clinical experience in such a way as to benefit their patients while they are advancing science."

Two Hundredth Anniversary

NOTES

1. "In the Preface to the fifth edition the author 'tenders his thanks to the present publishers for a continuance of the courtesy and kindness which rendered most agreeable his relations, for a quarter of a century, with their predecessors, Blanchard & Lea and Henry C. Lea.' Judging by the popular criterion of commercial success, the publishers can certainly testify to the appreciation, on the part of the profession, of the completeness with which each one of the preceding five editions has been made to represent the actual condition of medical knowledge at the time of its publication; and it may be safely asserted that during the last twenty years no systematic work on the *Principles and Practice of Medicine*, printed in the English language, has been more extensively circulated and read, and has had a greater influence on the practice of English-speaking physicians, than has the present treatise."

2. This collection of papers appeared originally in the *American Journal of the Medical Sciences* (itself a Lea publication whose origins go back to Mathew Carey's founding of the *Philadelphia Journal of the Medical and Physical Sciences* in 1820) and includes Edward H. Clarke, *Practical Medicine;* Henry J. Bigelow, *A History of the Discovery of Modern Anaesthesia;* Samuel D. Gross, *Surgery;* T. Gaillard Thomas, *Obstetrics and Gynecology;* and John S. Billings, *Literature and Institutions.*

3. It is best illustrated in Dunglison's account (in the *Autobiographical Ana*) of some of the fortunes of his phenomenal *Medical Lexicon:*

In the year 1851, it became necessary to prepare an eighth edition of the *Dictionary*, and propositions were made to me by my publishers to have it stereotyped. To this I objected for some time, but ultimately consented, provided that I should have the privilege of having the plates destroyed after a short period, so that the work should not suffer materially by its recomposition being delayed a little longer than had, thus far, been the case. The following arrangement was therefore entered into.

Philadelphia April 12th, 1851

Professor Dunglison
Dear Sir,
     It is understood, that we are to stereotype your revised copy of the *Medical Dictionary* and that you are not to require us to destroy or modify the plates, nor are we to require you to revise the work for a new edition, for a period of five years from the publication of the first fifteen hundred copies, (unless the said steel plates are accidentally injured or destroyed). Should we not have printed and sold *ten thousand copies* from the plates, at the expiration of the said five years, then, the understanding exists until the quantity of *ten thousand copies* are sold. The existing contract for this work, of accounting for each fifteen hundred copies, and other matters, are not affected by stereotyping it.
Yours very truly,

Blanchard and Lea

P.S. It is understood, that our selling price of the edition is not to be increased.

The following is an account of the number of copies and of the copy money paid to me for the *Dictionary* up to this date (June 1852):

Edition	Number of Copies	Copy Money
1833 First-	1000	$ 1250
1839 Second-	1500	$ 600
1842 Third-	1500	$ 900
1844 Fourth-	1500	$ 900
1845 Fifth-	1500	$ 900
1846 Sixth-	3750	$ 2250
1848 Seventh-	5000	$ 3000
1851 Eighth-	1500	$ 900
	17250	$10700

Henry Charles Lea

The Renaissance Man: Henry Charles Lea

V

Henry Charles Lea, born September 19, 1825, was truly a remarkable man, a Renaissance man, who was a giant despite his frail health and small stature. He and his brother, Matthew, were tutored in Isaac Lea's home, and both were excellent students, a trait that characterized their entire lives.[1] Henry learned the Greek alphabet from his mother at six, and went to Paris with his family at seven, where he laid the foundations for his mastery of French. In later years he learned Spanish, Italian, Portuguese, and German. At eighty he taught himself Dutch. He also had an extraordinary knowledge of Latin and some knowledge of Hebrew and Sanskrit.

Just after his fifteenth birthday, Henry contributed a paper on fossil shells to the *American Journal of Science and Arts* and soon followed that with a paper on the peroxide of manganese. His studious ways did not prevent him from having a happy childhood. He was fond of his brother and younger sister and had warm relationships with his many cousins, particularly Christian Febiger, whose son,

Christian Carson Febiger, Lea eventually brought into the firm. As a boy, he was often in the company of S. Weir Mitchell, the famous neurologist and prolific writer, who many years later was to have some of his books published by the firm.

Two Hundredth Anniversary

Henry Charles Lea had begun to work in the family firm in 1843. Lea confessed that he was not particularly fond of the publishing business and knew little about it, but in keeping with his nature, he spent long hours studying every aspect of it and soon mastered it. While working hard at the family business, he continued his studies and writings early in the morning and late into the night. In his early twenties he contributed a number of articles to various journals on such diverse subjects as conchology, Tennyson, and Greek epitaphs.

In 1847, at 22, his health broke down and then ensued what he described as a period of "intellectual leisure," during which he turned his attention to his life work as a historian. Free from the publishing business for a time, he traveled and became interested in French memoirs. He questioned the accuracy of some of the accounts he read and sent to Paris for books that might shed further light on the subjects about which he was reading. In 1858 his first historical work was published in the form of a book review in the *North American Review*. Following that date, Lea published a flood of articles, reviews, poems, political statements, and editorials in such magazines as *Lippincott's Magazine*, the *Nation, Atlantic,* and *The American Historical Review*. He was particularly fond of poetry, but recognized that he was not very good at composing it. An interest in early legal institutions gradually turned into an interest in the medieval church. In 1855 he published *Superstition and Force;* in 1867, *An Historical Sketch of Sacerdotal Celibacy;* and in 1869, *Studies in Church History.*

Philadelphia business had formed strong ties with the South (including the bookselling ties first forged by "Parson" Weems). Although much of the Philadelphia establishment was cool to the Union cause when the Civil War broke out, this was not the case with Henry C. Lea. An avid partisan of the Union and a strong critic of slavery,[2] he served on many committees and commissions set up to advance the cause of the Union. Philadelphia contained the largest black population in the North, and many of its citizens were prejudiced against them. In the midst of the war, Lea became a member of the staunchly antisecessionist Union League, for which he wrote many widely circulated pamphlets. He also served on a committee on "colored enlistments," which was a particularly difficult assignment because many Philadelphians looked askance at the enlistment of colored troops. In fact, when wounded black troops began to return from the front to be hospitalized in Philadelphia, the operators of the horsedrawn transportation lines for the most part refused to carry relatives to visit the wounded.[3]

His services to the Union led him to visit President Abraham Lincoln on several occasions. Lea was deeply impressed by Lincoln's intelligence and humanity. After the assassination, Lea wrote an eloquent tribute to Lincoln in a letter to a friend, Charles Eliot Norton.

Lea's house at 2000 Walnut Street, which housed his library built in 1869

"History presents many grander figures than that of Abraham Lincoln, but none who will preserve so firm a hold upon the affections of a people. His very weaknesses sprung from the traits which serve to attach a people to its ruler, while his uprightness and homely sagacity neutralized them in action. Had he been loftier he would have been less appreciated—and possibly less successful in his administration. It is singular that in our brief career we should have furnished to the world, in Washington and Lincoln, two perfect exemplars—one of the aristocratic and the other of democratic republicanism. His tragic end was all that was wanting to put the seal upon the tender remembrance with which he will be enshrined in our annals. I had three or four interviews with him last year and was much impressed with the kindly forbearance with which he strove to discharge the complicated duties of his office, and I believe that those loved him best who were brought most in contact with him. Peace be with him, for he has deserved well of his country and of mankind."

Two Hundredth Anniversary

At the end of the war Lea, an ardent Republican, cast aside his partisanship to organize the Municipal Reform Association to combat an orgy of Republican corruption in the city of Philadelphia. He was several times the President of that organization, and finally resigned from the Union League because it failed to denounce corruption to his satisfaction. He was an active member of the Committee of One Hundred—formed in 1880 and still existing—to clean up political corruption. His battle against corruption led him to become one of the first to support civil service reforms, and he wrote widely on the subject.

The evidence suggests that Henry Charles Lea enjoyed a warm family life. He and his wife, Anna

Henry C. Lea's library in his home

Caroline (Jaudon) Lea, had three sons—Francis Henry, Charles Matthew, Arthur Henry—and a daughter, Nina. Summers were spent at Cape May at his home on 9 Grant Street, while in early spring and autumn Lea customarily spent a few days at the Delaware Water Gap; at both places he particularly enjoyed the wild flowers, as botany was a pleasant diversion that he pursued throughout his life.

In recounting Henry C. Lea's many personal and civic pursuits, I have neglected the affairs of the company—something that Lea, himself, would never have done. In 1851, Isaac Lea retired in favor of his son, Henry, and the name of the firm became Blanchard & Lea. As described in the previous chapter, the firm prospered throughout the middle of the nineteenth century by publishing many outstanding medical books by prominent physician-teachers of the day, and Lea tied the publishing policy of the firm securely to medicine and closely related fields, even though he had some of his historical works published by his own firm. He carried on extensive and sympathetic correspondence with his authors, being particularly well equipped to see both author and publisher viewpoints.[4] As an author and a publisher he also had good reason to be interested in international copyright. Like his predecessors, he opposed literary piracy, and welcomed an opportunity to play a major role in developing the first international copyright law passed by the United States. After 10 years of debate and several unsatisfactory bills, the Congress passed the Chace bill in 1891, which was mainly written by Henry C. Lea, in whom Senator Chace had full confidence.

Nineteenth century ledger. The firm used similar ledgers until a few years ago

Under Lea, in the year 1859, the firm made a decision by which it has profited for well over 100 years. Upon learning of the publication of *Gray's Anatomy* in London, Blanchard and Lea made immediate arrangements with Gray's London publisher, Parker, for rights to publish the *Anatomy* on this side of the Atlantic and imported a complete set of wood blocks for the illustrations. This first American edition was published in June, 1859 and the 30th American edition, in 1985.

Two Hundredth Anniversary

In 1865 Blanchard retired after a connection with the house that had lasted for more than half a century. His place was taken by his son, Henry, and for a short time the firm again became Lea & Blanchard. According to Bradley, Lea's biographer, Lea offered Blanchard a choice of selling his partnership or buying Lea's, but after a few months Blanchard's health began to fail and he decided to sell, which was probably a bit disappointing to Lea, who had looked forward to spending more time on his various researches and writings. In 1880 Lea's own health began to decline, and he formed the firm of Henry C. Lea's Son and Company, bringing into partnership his son, Charles M. Lea, and a long-time employee, Henry M. Barnes.[5] Though remaining a special partner until 1885, Lea in effect retired from the business.

His health led Henry C. Lea to consult S. Weir Mitchell, who prescribed a "schedule of life" to which Lea conformed rigidly and thus was enabled to prolong his work for many more years. Each morning he took a long walk, which gave him an opportunity to look over his extensive real estate holdings. The remainder of the day was spent in

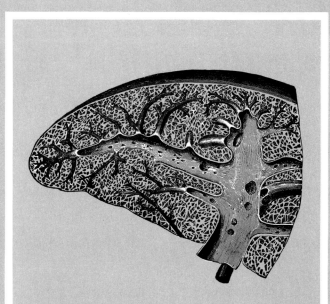

Transverse section of the spleen, from Henry Gray, 1854. This illustration has been published in all American editions of Gray's Anatomy. *The text of the section on the spleen describing various physical dimensions according to age, race, nutritional status, and health is taken from a monograph titled* The Structure and Use of the Spleen, *published by Gray in 1854, which won the triennial Astley Cooper Prize of £300 in 1853.*

Each new edition of Gray's Anatomy, *although revised, continues the fine tradition of its remarkable originator and reflects the groundwork he laid for the first edition.*

revising his notes, planning his work, or reading proof. He customarily wrote from after dinner until midnight.

Lea's "retirement" led to what can best be described as an orgy of work and study. He made it a rule to work from original sources and kept copyists busy in several of the great archives of Europe (particularly Spain) and South America. He borrowed heavily from some of Europe's leading libraries, which led Benjamin Disraeli to remark that Mr. Lea was stripping the libraries of Europe, an allegation indignantly denied by Lea. He never had a secretary or dictated a letter; everything he wrote was done in his own meticulous hand. Once, when asked if he really enjoyed what appeared to others to be unremitting drudgery, he replied that there was no pleasure equal to it.

Two Hundredth Anniversary

In 1888 he published his masterpiece, the three-volume *History of the Inquisition of the Middle Ages.* In rapid succession there followed *Chapters from the Religious History of Spain Connected with the Inquisition* (1890); *A Formulary of the Papal Penitentiary in the Thirteenth Century* (1892), which he edited; a three-volume *History of Auricular Confession and Indulgences* (1896); *The Moriscos of Spain: Their Conversion and Expulsion* (1901); *A History of the Inquisition of Spain* (1906–1907); *The Inquisition in the Spanish Dependencies* (1908).[6]

Many honors came his way. Lea was made a Fellow of the Imperial University of Moscow and an honorary member of learned societies in Germany, Italy, and Great Britian. He was elected to the

American Academy of Arts and Letters and the American Philosophical Society. The American Historical Association elected him President, and Harvard, Pennsylvania, Princeton, and the University of Giessen awarded him degrees. The Catholic historian, Lord Acton, praised his even-handed, unbiased treatment of the Inquisition, and invited him to contribute an important chapter to the first volume of the *Cambridge Modern History*. His friend, the historian, James Bryce, called Lea one of the three greatest scholars in the world and sought, unsuccessfully, Lea's help in writing *The American Commonwealth*.

Two Hundredth Anniversary

Lea remained modest in the face of such praise. When 81, he wrote: "As regards an autobiography, I am like Canning's knife-grinder—Story, Lord bless you sir, I've none to tell. I only followed my convictions and worked as they led me. Besides, I have no time to waste. Every day shortens the little term left to me and I have two books under way . . . so you see my program is a pretty full one, especially as age is beginning to tell on me, and I find that my power of labor is not what it was a half-century ago."

On October 20, 1909, while working on a volume on the history of witchcraft, he was taken with a severe chill. He placed his pen as a marker in the book he was reading, planning to return to his work the next day. Four days later, in his eighty-fifth year, he died of pneumonia despite the ministrations of his physician, Hobard Amory Hare, a Lea author. His good friend, the Reverend Dr. Joseph May, Pastor of the First Unitarian Church of Philadelphia,

93

conducted a simple funeral service in the Lea house on Walnut Street. The multi-volume history of witchcraft was finally published in 1938.

Lea's considerable wealth benefited the Institute of Hygiene at the University of Pennsylvania, a farm for epileptics, and the Jefferson Medical School. The impressive Lea Library at the University of Pennsylvania was donated in 1926 by Lea's children in accordance with his will.

Two Hundredth Anniversary

NOTES

1. Matthew was two years Henry's senior. He had an extraordinarily quick mind and eventually read law and was admitted to the bar. He never practiced however, but turned to chemistry, a field in which he made many contributions, particularly as it related to photography. His book, *Manual of Photography*, was long a standard reference. A member of the American Academy of Sciences, he died in 1897.

2. This was not the first time Lea opposed popular prejudice. In 1844 vicious anti-Catholic rioting broke out in Philadelphia and two churches were burned down. The slight young man, Henry C. Lea, shouldered a gun and stood guard for two days at St. Patrick's Church on Locust Street.

3. Russell F. Weigley, Professor of History at Temple University, is the source for this information. A full account of this problem may be read in the July and October, 1973, issues of *Pennsylvania History*. Racism dies hard: in World War II the National Guard had to be called in when blacks were hired as motormen on Philadelphia streetcars.

4. Lea wrote to the historian, W. E. H. Lecky:

"As a rule, I do not think well of publishing on commission. While I was in business I always refused to undertake it, for I rated my time and facilities high and I never would invest them where I would hesitate to invest capital. I always had more capital than I could employ, while I was limited to the working hours of a day. The author moreover will get better work out of a publisher who has his capital involved and must labor to get it out. It is in human nature that his efforts should be directed where his interests are greatest. The fairest method on both sides I think is the payment of a royalty of copy money on sales, which in this country has settled itself at ten per cent of the retail price, equivalent to about fifteen on the wholesale price.

"There is one ineradicable trouble in the publishing business. In order to carry it on the publisher must necessarily make the good books carry the bad, and not more than twenty or twenty-five per cent of the books published are "good" commercially. The author of a successful book is naturally discontented that a part of what he regards as his lawful gains should be diverted to make up for the losses accruing from unsuccessful books, and the authors of the latter are discontented that their works are unsuccessful. It is a speculative business throughout, and the most experienced sagacity is at fault in foretelling the result of each single book."

Two Hundredth Anniversary

5. Barnes became the third man in the company's history to be named a partner who was not related to the family by blood or marriage. William Blanchard was the first, and he was followed for a few short months by his son, Henry Blanchard.

6. E. S. Bradley's *Henry Charles Lea* contains the full list of Lea's writings for those who are interested. Incidentally, Lea's *History of the Inquisition of Spain* was originally written to make up eight volumes. In 1905, at age 80, Lea decided it was too long and reduced it to four volumes. The work of pruning and paraphrasing was done by Lea with pen and ink.

Christian Carson Febiger

VI

Upon Henry C. Lea's final retirement in January,
1885, the firm once again went through one of its
ritualistic name changes. Henry C. Lea's son, Arthur
H. Lea, was admitted to the partnership and its
name became Lea Brothers & Co. The last and, we
hope, final name change occurred in 1908 when
these partners, Charles M. Lea, Christian Carson
Febiger,[1] and Arthur H. Lea changed to the name
Lea & Febiger. They could count among their
successes the publication of William Osler's
seven-volume set, *Modern Medicine, Its Theory and
Practice.* Osler was a world-famous clinician and
pathologist who, along with other such luminaries
as John Shaw Billings and William S. Halstead, at
the Johns Hopkins Hospital and School of Medicine
in 1889, was instrumental in establishing medical
education in America as we know it today, with two
years of graduate study in the sciences, two years of

NOV 26 1915

161.

13, NORHAM GARDENS,
OXFORD.

Dear Sirs

Yes please —
send cheque to Dominion
Bank — Head Office
Toronto.

I do hope that Modern
Medicine has been a
success financially. It
has been a great pleasure
to have my name
associated with a pub-
lication of your firm.

Why wish you had had
my text book!

Greetings & regards to you
all

Sincerely yours

Wm Osler

Letter from William Osler

Christian Febiger

internship in hospital practice, and postgraduate specialization by "resident" physicians who lived in the hospital itself. Lea Brothers had long courted Osler, publishing his articles in *The American Journal of the Medical Sciences* and corresponding with him before he moved to Philadelphia in 1884 to succeed to the chair vacated by another Lea author, William Pepper, Professor of Clinical Medicine at the University of Pennsylvania. Despite their efforts, the firm failed to land the big prize— Osler's *Textbook of Medicine*, which he published with Appleton. Nonetheless, *Modern Medicine* went through three editions: the first volume appeared in 1907; the second, in 1913; and the third, in 1925. Thomas McCrae assisted Osler in all three editions. Osler sometimes had second thoughts about his choice of publisher for his *Textbook*, as indicated by his letter received November 26, 1915: "Yes please—send cheque to Dominion Bank—head office Toronto. I do hope that Modern Medicine has been a success financially. It has been a great pleasure to have my name associated with a publication of your firm. I wish you had had my textbook!"

Charles Lea, Christian Carson Febiger, and Arthur Lea all retired in 1915. The business was carried on by Van Antwerp Lea, great-great-grandson of Mathew Carey, and Christian Febiger, son of Christian Carson Febiger. These two men worked well enough together as partners, with Mr. Lea assuming most of the editorial responsibility and Mr. Febiger taking care of the financial side of the business. Their personal relationship, however, was cool, and on one occasion Mr. Lea left a note on Mr. Febiger's desk offering to buy him out.

Two Hundredth Anniversary

The partnership of Van Antwerp Lea and Christian Febiger had a decidedly cautious approach to publishing. They gradually phased out the few nursing titles that the firm had acquired. They let die those titles of a nonmedical nature that had lingered from earlier times, such as the 24-volume set, *History of All Nations*, first published in 1902 and in a second edition in 1905. At the same time they had the foresight to begin a line of dental hygiene books by publishing the first such book of its kind, Fones' *Mouth Hygiene*, put out in an edition of 1,500 copies in 1916. Today the firm is the premier publisher in dental hygiene, with Esther Wilkins' *Clinical Practice of the Dental Hygienist* leading the list.

Two Hundredth Anniversary

Further, under their management in the 30s and 40s, the firm signed some impressive medical and dental titles that continue to bolster the company's treasury to this day. Chief among these books were Wintrobe's *Clinical Hematology*,[2] William Boyd's *Textbook of Pathology*, *Pathology of Internal Diseases*, and *Introduction to the Study of Disease*,[3] Craig and Faust's *Clinical Parasitology*, Comroe's *Arthritis* (now McCarty's), and Louis Grossman's *Endodontic Practice*.[4]

Lea & Febiger had a rather Dickensian appearance in those days. Smoking was allowed, but only in the lavatories. Gentlemen were expected to wear hats when reporting for work, and during the Depression, employees were often asked to hand deliver letters to save on postage. Roll-top and stand-up desks of a great age were much in evidence, and many of the loyal employees were of an age to match the desks.

Among those long-time employees was W. D. Wilcox, an excellent acquisitions editor who traveled the country signing new authors and visiting established ones. He was careful of his own money and his employer's as well, preferring to pick up a morning newspaper abandoned in the hotel lobby by a fellow traveler rather than buying his own. In charge of relations with wholesale and retail booksellers and also the head of the shipping room was Fred Sauers, who stayed with the company 61 years and trained many of the younger employees, including Richard Foster. Mr. Foster, who worked for the firm during the Depression, first as a shipping clerk, then as an acquisitions editor, eventually left Lea & Febiger to establish the Rittenhouse Book Distributors, a major medical book wholesaler.

In 1945 Christian Febiger toppled from a New Jersey train platform, the victim of a stroke. He died shortly thereafter, gaining the unhappy distinction of being the first partner to die in the course of his partnership. Van Antwerp Lea continued alone through the remainder of the year.

In 1946, Mr. Lea invited his cousin, Henry Lea Hudson, and Christian Febiger's nephews, Christian Carson Febiger Spahr and John Febiger Spahr, to share in the partnership. Nine years later, Van Antwerp Lea prepared for retirement by selling half of his share to his nephew, Francis Carey Lea, Jr. In 1957 he sold his remaining share to another nephew, F. Woodson Hancock, and retired to his baronial home in Chestnut Hill. Mr. Lea, who never married, was a shy, quiet, and introverted man, but doubtless a kind one, for when it was suggested in

Van Antwerp Lea

his later years that he divest himself of the burdens of his enormous house, which he had purchased from the estate of Arthur Lea, he demurred by saying, "What would happen to the servants?"

Once again, in January, 1962, a reorganization of the partnership came about when Francis Carey Lea, Jr. bought out the one-eighth share owned by F. Woodson Hancock, Jr., who left the publishing field. Francis Carey Lea, Jr., along with Henry Lea Hudson and the brothers, Christian and John Spahr, then became equal partners until December 31, 1968, when Henry Lea Hudson retired.

Hudson contributed much to the firm. A graduate of Harvard University, he came to Lea & Febiger in 1932 and spent many of his earlier years traveling extensively throughout the United States and Canada acquiring manuscripts. His relationship with the firm was interrupted during World War II while he served in the U.S. Army in India. Upon his return from service he rejoined Lea & Febiger and became a partner in 1946. At that time he assumed the role of editor-in-chief, thus continuing his long relationship with many of Lea & Febiger's authors.

A considerate man, he left his money in the firm after his retirement until such time as the remaining partners were better able to purchase his share. Hudson retired to his Paoli home and passed away on January 26, 1982 at the age of 75.

Upon Mr. Hudson's retirement, John F. Spahr became editor-in-chief as well as the partner in charge of production, and the firm continued under three partners until January 1, 1972, when

Christian C. F. Spahr, Jr. acquired Mr. Hudson's share. Thus the partnership, as of this writing, consists of Christian C. F. Spahr, John F. Spahr, Francis Carey Lea, Jr., and Christian C. F. Spahr, Jr.—each having one-fourth ownership.

The partnerships that followed that of Van Antwerp Lea and Christian Febiger proceeded to relax some of the 19th century approaches to business and office routine. While holding on to many of the company's more cherished and charming traditions, they reluctantly cut loose the long-lived and celebrated—but financially ailing—*American Journal of the Medical Sciences.* Employee benefits such as a pension plan, health insurance, and vacations tied to length of service were instituted, and in a rather touching development, the company added a turkey to the customary Christmas cash bonus for each employee. The firm gave added attention to its foreign trade and to stepping up its attempts to sell translation rights. In 1970 Lea & Febiger established *The Henry Gray Award,* which is a cash award presented annually by The American Association of Anatomists to "an individual in recognition of sustained and meritorious service to the entire scientific community through scholarly accomplishments in original investigation, teaching, and writing in the field of Anatomy." A copyediting department was set up and the advertising and promotion department was strengthened, as was the college department, which is that part of the firm involved in seeking adoptions for textbooks. The offices were given a much needed refurbishing, which had to be repeated in 1980 when a fire swept through the front part of the second floor, doing extensive

Two Hundredth Anniversary

Important

Dear Doctor:

The important announcement appearing a few lines below, together with the analysis of three issues, is deserving of your thoughtful consideration.

The American Journal of the Medical Sciences is the preferred magazine of the big men of the profession, it is one of the most constantly consulted mediums in libraries. From 4 to 10 copies go monthly to such medical centers as Johns Hopkins, Mayo Clinic, Rockefeller Institute and our biggest colleges and hospitals. WHY! *Because the value is there.* If it can help and be of value to such men and such institutions it is reasonable to assert that you would likewise find it a paying investment.

Announcement for March

THE ROLE OF FAT IN DIABETES. By FREDERICK M. ALLEN, M.D., of the Rockefeller Institute.

A vitally important and little understood phase of the diabetic problem is discussed from every angle by the man who has revolutionized the clinical management of Diabetes and given us the only successful method of controlling the disease. It amounts to a monograph, taking up practically 60 pages. When we originally announced Dr. Allen's Fasting Treatment for Diabetes in October, 1915, the demand from all over the world was so great that the edition was sold out in a week. The present article is equally important. DON'T MISS IT.

Endothelioma of the Right Bronchus Removed by Peroral Bronchoscopy. By CHEVALIER JACKSON, Professor of Laryngology, Jefferson Medical College.

A clinical paper of interest, particularly to the laryngologist, written by the greatest authority on bronchoscopy in the United States.

Spelter Chills. By DAVID RIESMAN, M.D., Professor of Clinical Medicine, University of Pennsylvania, and RUSSELL S. BOLES, M.D., Philadelphia.

This paper is especially important in view of the present-day interest in occupational diseases and industrial hygiene. It describes a hitherto little understood type of zinc poisoning found among certain brass workers, and outlines the precautions necessary to prevent this form of acute intoxication.

Unilateral Renal Hypoplasia and Dysplasia due to Defective Arteriogenesis; Relation to So-called Hypogenetic Nephritis. By W. M. L. COPLIN, M.D., Prof. of Pathology, Jefferson Medical College.

A careful, pathological study by one of the country's leading pathologists of an important condition too infrequently recognized clinically. The subject has a definite clinical as well as pathological interest.

A 1917 mailing piece

The Rarity of Conjugal Phthisis. By MAURICE FISHBERG, M.D., Clinical Professor of Medicine, New York University and Bellevue Hospital.

The author of this paper has devoted much time and care to the study of tuberculosis and is recognized as one of our most eminent authorities. He gives some important conclusions in regard to the transmissibility of this disease.

The Status of Diphtheroids with Special Reference to Hodgkin's Disease. By W. F. CUNNINGHAM, M.D., Pathological Lab., Roosevelt Hos.

The Etiology of Hodgkin's disease has occasioned much discussion. This article disposes of one factor of alleged etiological importance.

The Invasive Quality of the Streptococci in the Living Animal. By W. L. HOLMAN, M.D., Pathological Laboratories, Univ. of Pittsburgh.

Observations Upon a Case of Extreme Acidosis Occurring in a Man with Bilateral Cystic Kidneys. By J. H. MEANS, M.D., Harvard University, and O. F. ROGERS.

Effect of Nuclean Injection upon the Leukocytes of Dogs. By HERBERT FOX, M.D., Pepper Lab., Univ. of Penna., and F. B. LYNCH, M.D.

Familial Epistaxis; A Case Report. By HENRY B. RICHARDSON, M.D., Peter Bent Brigham Hospital, Boston, Mass.

Four articles of decided clinical and pathological interest; of value alike to the practising physician and laboratory worker.

WEIGH THIS ISSUE and the others described on the following pages. Bear in mind this journal's century-old reputation of being the first to publish the big and important medical discoveries and of getting the big articles from the big men, the leaders in every field of medicine and surgery.

January

*S*e*V*e*n* noteworthy articles on *Metabolism, Acidosis and Diabetes* in a single issue is distinctly an achievement. These with equally valuable articles on other subjects make a number of great clinical value.

damage. The shipping room and stock area were removed to a new building from congested quarters in the office building. The computer replaced the quill pen.

In the face of fierce and growing competition for new manuscripts, from both old and newly established medical publishers, the partners strengthened their staff of acquisition editors. Among the several worthy editors hired in the 1940s and 1950s, Charles Moritz stands out. Moritz, a Ph.D. in Zoology, played a significant role in strengthening the company's pharmacy and veterinary line of books and was responsible for adding two of the firm's best selling titles, *An Atlas of Human Histology* by diFiore and *Functional Human Anatomy* by James Crouch.[5]

The company also hired Dr. Ruth Abernathy, Professor Emeritus, School of Physical and Health Education at the University of Washington, as Editorial Adviser, charged with helping obtain a series of books in health education, physical education, and recreation. Many of the successful books Lea & Febiger continues to publish in this area were first recommended by Dr. Abernathy.

To list some of the books of merit published under the aegis of the partners who followed Van Antwerp Lea is to court the disfavor of many unlisted, but nonetheless worthy, authors in the firm's catalog. I will take that risk.

In the past thirty years Lea & Febiger has been proud to publish *Merritt's A Textbook of Neurology;* Goodhart, Shils, and Young: *Modern Nutrition in*

108

The partnership in 1953. (From left to right standing)
Christian C. Febiger Spahr, Henry Lea Hudson, John
Febiger Spahr. (Seated) Van Antwerp Lea.

Health and Disease; Jones and Hunt: *Veterinary Pathology*; Feigenbaum: *Echocardiography*; Ingle: *Endodontics*; Holland and Frei: *Cancer Medicine*; Menkes: *Child Neurology*; Petrak: *Diseases of Cage and Aviary Birds*; Adams: *Lameness in Horses*; Martin, Swarbrick, and Cammarata: *Physical Pharmacy*; Foye: *Principles of Medicinal Chemistry*; Hansten: *Drug Interactions*; Ackerman: *Histologic Diagnosis of Inflammatory Skin Diseases*; Weyman: *Cross-Sectional Echocardiography*; and McArdle, Katch, and Katch: *Exercise Physiology*.

All of the foregoing have been successful—some to a remarkable degree. More importantly, they are books of merit, worthy of a statement Lea & Febiger and its predecessor firms put on its title pages for over a hundred years: "Quae Prosunt Omnibus"—that which benefits all.

NOTES

1. Christian C. Febiger, born April 2, 1845, was the son of Christian Febiger and Sarah Tatnall. The Febigers were descendants of a Revolutionary War colonel who emigrated from Denmark. Christian C. Febiger came to work for the firm in 1865, became a partner in 1880, and retired in 1915. He died in August, 1930. His obituary in the *Philadelphia Public Ledger* noted that he was a director on boards of banks, coal companies, railroads, iron and steel companies, as well as President of the Philadelphia Zoo. His work at Lea & Febiger was primarily involved with the financial side of the business. He was a hunter and fisherman of note, and continued his enthusiasm for fishing until extreme old age.

2. Dr. Wintrobe recounted his association with the firm in a letter written July 27, 1981:

"*Clinical Hematology* developed out of work I had done with John H. Musser, who had been my chief at Tulane, 1927 to 1930. John Musser

Lea & Febiger partners in 1984. (From left to right)
Christian C. Febiger Spahr, John Febiger Spahr,
Francis Carey Lea, Jr., and Christian C. Febiger
Spahr, Jr.

William Boyd

Louis I. Grossman

Maxwell M. Wintrobe

Mariano S.H. diFiore

James E. Crouch

Charles M. Goss

Esther Wilkins

Carmine D. Clemente

was the son of John Musser, Sr., whose textbook, as I recall, you [Lea & Febiger] had published. I believe the family was an old Philadelphia family. Not long after I had arrived in New Orleans (coming there from Winnipeg), Dr. Musser was asked to revise the section on diseases of the blood in the *Tice Practice of Medicine*. Since, by this time, I had manifested an interest in blood, Dr. Musser asked if I would be interested in revising the Tice material with him. He said that no doubt I would have to do half the work or more but that he would edit what I prepared and would do as much as he could himself. He also stated that if I did not feel that I would like to do this, he would turn down the request as he did not have time enough to do it all himself. . . . I agreed because I had nothing to lose and much to gain, and got to work. As predicted, I did most of the work but that did not bother me. I learned a great deal by reviewing all the literature.

"The Tice people provided us with 250 reprints of the section on blood which, incidentally, turned out to be quite sizeable. I gave copies to my friends and the comments were quite favorable. As time went on, the section had to be revised and I did more and more of this, ultimately doing it all and, ultimately, with my name alone as the author. I continued to send reprints to my friends and associates and people began to suggest that I prepare a book on hematology. There was nothing entirely satisfactory in the English language. . . . I did begin to work in the late 1930s on the project and, as I recall, I showed a copy of the first chapter to [W. B.] Saunders [Company]. They responded by saying that they thought they might be interested in publishing such a book, but they had one very important piece of advice for me. They thought that the numerous references I had were superfluous. They *knew* that physicians did not want all that sort of material. They simply were interested in the text.

"I responded that I had no interest in writing the sort of thing they wanted. I did not believe in writers saying 'this is what *I* think' and leaving it at that. It was my impression that this was the German approach and I had no sympathy with it. My training had been to ask why and what the grounds were for the statements that were made, and I felt that any thinking physician would want to know the basis for any statement I would make."

"I wrote Dr. Musser about all this and he, in turn, wrote to Lea & Febiger and suggested that they would be well advised to look at my proposal sympathetically. This they did, and so a project which is now reaching its 40th year was launched."

The editor that Dr. Musser contacted was Richard Foster, who in turn visited Dr. Wintrobe. Discussions got underway and in time Henry Lea Hudson became involved and encouraged Dr. Wintrobe to contract with Lea & Febiger.

3. William Boyd offered his pathology textbook to Mr. Ryland Greene of W. B. Saunders in 1931. Saunders already published a textbook of pathology, so Mr. Greene kindly walked Dr. Boyd across Washington Square to Lea & Febiger's office, and the rest is medical publishing history. Boyd's highly successful books, along with Wintrobe's *Textbook of Hematology*, played a major role in keeping the firm financially healthy during the Depression.

Two Hundredth Anniversary

4. Grossman's book was the first successful text in endodontia. The first unsuccessful text in endodontia was published by Lea & Febiger in October, 1920. Entitled *Root Canal Therapy* by Crane, the book sold for $2.25. Grossman recalled the beginning of his book in this letter:

"The contact with Lea & Febiger was made through Mr. W. D. Wilcox of your firm. I believe he was called College Editor at the time. Both Mr. Wilcox and his wife, Dixie, became patients at my private office soon after they came to this city from Chicago.

"I had been accumulating notes for a book on root canal treatment for about a decade. Since 1926 I had been teaching endodontics at the University of Pennsylvania and many of the notes had been saved with the object of eventually writing a book. To prepare myself toward that end I took a two-month course in general pathology at Harvard Medical School in 1937. In 1938 my wife and I took a cottage for the better part of two months in Bermuda during which time I hammered together the book. The finishing touches were put on the manuscript during the next few months at home.

"When confronted with the manuscript, Mr. Wilcox advised me that Lea & Febiger had previously published a book on the subject of root canal treatment which had not been financially successful. He assured me that he would do his utmost to recommend its publication. The first edition appeared in 1940 and the tenth in 1981. The book, *Endodontic Practice*, has been published at various times in Spanish, Portuguese, German, Italian, Chinese, Japanese, and Persian. It has also been translated into Turkish."

5. Crouch's remembrance of his first encounter with Lea & Febiger follows:

"My first acquaintance with Lea & Febiger was through the use of some of your books in my teaching at San Diego University. *Gray's Anatomy* was my constant companion.

"Charlie Moritz, who was my friend and colleague for a number of years, later went to Lea & Febiger as one of the editors. We continued our friendship, and on many occasions when he was in San Diego in his official capacity as editor, he urged me to write an elementary human anatomy book. He had a strong feeling that undergraduate textbooks should be written by instructors of undergraduates whose primary concern was good teaching. His persistence was greater than my resistance to the idea, so I wrote the book—*Functional Human Anatomy*. My resistance was due mostly to my feeling that I might not be the proper and best qualified person to do the book, not because I feared the hard work. I'm happy that Charlie won. It has enabled me to add many dimensions to the life of my family—world travel and the like.

"My contract called for a book of 350 pages, as I recall, and the book turned out to be over 600 pages, which Charlie said worried people at Lea & Febiger. I wrote it much as I taught it and as I felt it—leaving out the corny jokes. The writing was quite easy, much more so than I expected, but getting the illustrations was a most difficult task, and hence the many illustrators used and the unevenness in the quality of illustrations in the first edition. Yet it sold and all involved were much relieved."

L'Envoi

Today, in its 200th year, the firm, remaining true to its long heritage, continues to be a partnership. Christian Carson Febiger Spahr, John Febiger Spahr, Francis Carey Lea, Jr., and Christian Carson Febiger Spahr, Jr. are co-equal partners. Chris and Jack are the grandchildren of the former partner, Christian Carson Febiger, and Francis Carey Lea, Jr. is the great-great-great grandson of Mathew Carey.

Customarily the firm publishes between 35 and 50 new titles and new editions per year. About half of the company's titles (providing about half of its income) are medical books. The other books are in the fields of dentistry, pharmacy, dental hygiene, physical education, health and recreation, animal science, and veterinary medicine. An important but relatively small number of titles are in biology. The company employs approximately 55 people in Philadelphia, and is still ensconced at 600 Washington Square, in the building that was erected in 1923. It warehouses and ships its books from a massive building at 6808 Greenway Avenue, Philadelphia, which it shares with Murphy-Parker, a binder responsible for most Lea & Febiger bindings. The company's typesetting is done by several firms, chief among which are William J. Dornan, Inc., and York Graphic Services, who typeset this book. Most of Lea & Febiger's printing is done by William J. Dornan, which was started in 1877 with the financial help of Henry C. Lea. Additionally, the company has contracts with people in other countries to promote our books and to encourage the translation of our titles into languages other than English. A world-wide network of agencies, booksellers, wholesalers, and warehousing operations handle Lea & Febiger books in other nations.

Two Hundredth Anniversary

In anticipation of future partnerships to come, John Febiger Spahr, Jr. is an employee of the firm. That there will be future partnerships is devoutly to be wished (but Heaven forbid any future name changes), and it is hoped that this text will prove useful to whomever is charged with writing the next anniversary history of the firm.

Bibliography

Billings, J. S.: *Literature and Institutions.* In
A Century of American Medicine, 1776–1876.
Philadelphia, Henry C. Lea, 1876.

Bishop, M.: "Parson Weems, Virtue's
Recruiting-Sergeant." *The New Yorker,* Vol. XII,
(No. 1), February 22, 1936.

Bradley, E. S.: *Henry Charles Lea: A Biography.*
Philadelphia, University of Pennsylvania Press,
1931.

Bradsher, E. L.: *Mathew Carey: Editor, Author and
Publisher. A Study in American Literary
Development.* New York, Columbia University
Press, 1912.

Carey, M.: *Autobiography.* New York, Research
Classics, No. 1, 1942.

Cordasco, F.: *American Medical Imprints,
1820–1910: A Check-list of Publications
Illustrating the History and Progress of Medical
Science, Medical Education, and the Healing
Arts in the United States.* In preparation.

Cushing, H.: *The Life of Sir William Osler*. New York, Oxford University Press, 1940.

Dictionary of American Biography. New York, Charles Scribner's Sons, 1934.

Gross, S. D.: *Autobiography of Samuel D. Gross, M.D., with Sketches of His Contemporaries*. Edited by his sons. 2 vols. Philadelphia, George Barrie, Publisher, 1887.

Henry, F. P. (Ed.): *Standard History of the Medical Profession of Philadelphia*. Chicago, Goodspeed, 1897.

Johnson, A.: *A Rage for Reason: A Study of Mathew Carey*. Unpublished manuscript.

Kaser, D.: "Chronology of Carey Imprints." Papers of the Bibliographical Society of America (New York), Vol. 50(No. 1): 190–193, 1956.

Kaser, D. (Ed.): *The Cost Book of Carey & Lea, 1825–1838*. Philadelphia, University of Pennsylvania Press, 1963.

Landis, H. R. M.: *The History of the Development of Medical Science in America*. Philadelphia, Lea Brothers, 1901.

[Lea & Febiger:] *One Hundred and Fifty Years of Publishing, 1785–1935*. Philadelphia, Lea & Febiger, 1935.

Lea, H. C.: *Minor Historical Writings and Other Essays*. Edited by Arthur C. Howland. Port Washington, N.Y., Kennikat Press, 1942.

Henry Charles Lea, 1825–1909. Philadelphia, Privately Printed, 1910.

Two Hundredth Anniversary

Morton, L. T.: *A Medical Bibliography (Garrison-Morton): An Annotated Check-list of Texts Illustrating the History of Medicine.* 3rd ed. Philadelphia, J. B. Lippincott Co., 1970.

Sellers, E. J.: *Jaudon Family of Pennsylvania.* Philadelphia, Privately Printed, 1924.

Skeel, E. E. F.: Mason Locke Weems. 3 Vols. New York, Privately Printed, 1929.

Tebbel, J.: *A History of Book Publishing in the United States.* 4 Vols. New York, R. R. Bowker, 1972.

Weigley. R. F. (Ed.): *Philadelphia: A 300-Year History.* New York, W. W. Norton, 1982.

Wolfe, G. R.: *The House of Appleton.* Metuchen, N. J., The Scarecrow Press, Inc., 1981.

Two Hundredth Anniversary

Index of Names

Page numbers in *italics* indicate illustrations; page numbers followed by "n" indicate notes.

125

Colophon

This limited edition of
Two Hundred Years of Publishing
by R. Kenneth Bussy was designed by Howard N. King.

The phototype is eleven on thirteen Zapf Book,
set by York Graphic Services, Inc.
Offset printing by William J. Dornan, Inc.
on Lustro Offset Enamel.
Bound by Murphy-Parker, Inc.

All for the joy of doing.

M. CAREY AND COMPANY
January 25, 1785 — March 25, 1785

CAREY, TALBOT AND SPOTSWOOD
March 26, 1785 — February 14, 1787

MATHEW CAREY AND COMPANY
February 15, 1787 — December 31, 1789

CAREY, STEWART & COMPANY
January 1, 1790 — December 31, 1791

M. CAREY
January 1, 1792 — December 31, 1816

M. CAREY & SON
January 1, 1817 — April 23, 1821

M. CAREY & SONS
April 24, 1821— December 31, 1821

H. C. CAREY & I. LEA
January 1, 1822 — April 9, 1827

CAREY, LEA & CAREY
April 10, 1827 — November 1, 1829

CAREY & LEA
November 2, 1829 — December 31, 1832

CAREY, LEA & BLANCHARD
January 1, 1833 — September 30, 1838

LEA & BLANCHARD
October 1, 1838 — December 31, 1850